OUR FAVOURITE FOOD

As voted for
by the members of
Friends Reunited

Marks and Spencer p.l.c.
PO Box 3339
Chester CH99 9QS

www.marksandspencer.com

ISBN: 1-84461-176-0
T21/8285/5329B

Printed in Dubai

Produced by The Bridgewater Book Company Ltd.

NOTES FOR THE READER

- This book uses both metric and imperial measurements. Follow the same units
  of measurement throughout; do not mix metric and imperial.

- All spoon measurements are level: teaspoons are assumed to be 5 ml, and
  tablespoons are assumed to be 15 ml.

- Unless otherwise stated, milk is assumed to be full fat, eggs and individual vegetables
  such as potatoes are medium, and pepper is freshly ground black pepper.

- Recipes using raw or very lightly cooked eggs should be avoided by infants, the
  elderly, pregnant women, convalescents and anyone suffering from an illness.

- The times given are an approximate guide only. Preparation times differ according
  to the techniques used by different people and the cooking times may also vary
  from those given.

Contents

Introduction

Friends and food go together like apple pie and custard or chicken tikka and a pint of lager. Whether a sophisticated dinner party or a tray of pick-and-mix snacks, sharing food with our nearest and dearest is one of the most basic human instincts found in every country and culture across the globe. So the Friends Reunited website was, in many ways, the obvious place to go to find out what our favourite food really is.

> " I love having friends round for meals and any excuse will do. Twelve of us once celebrated the invention of Wellington boots. "
>
> *Linda, Shepherds Bush*

With over 16 million people listed, Friends Reunited not only makes it easy to find old friends, it also offers the thoughts and views of an amazing cross-section of the British people. Our survey received responses from people of all ages, and from all areas and backgrounds, making it a true reflection of the nation's tastes. Visitors to the site were asked to vote for their favourite dishes in six categories designed to reflect today's varied lifestyles: Like Mother Used to Make, Dinner Party Dazzlers, Everyday Essentials, Friday Night Specials, Holiday Romance and New Wave. The choice was extensive, ranging from quick and easy salads to classics of international cuisine and from simple, inexpensive dishes to luxurious and self-indulgent treats. Each category included three further sub-sections: light meals, main courses and desserts, to make choosing easier and to provide an even more detailed picture of what the nation really likes to eat.

How we voted

It should be no surprise to anyone that many traditional British dishes scored highly – and not just in the Like Mother Used to Make category. We really do love our English breakfast, prawn cocktail, roast dinner and jam roly poly. The best of British cooking rightly occupies a place in our hearts and on our tables. However, living in such a diverse society has shaped our tastes to include dishes from all over the world. Indian curries, whether meat or vegetarian, and Chinese specialities, such as chow mein and spring rolls, gained huge support, but were closely followed by dishes reflecting many of our other communities from Caribbean jerk chicken to Thai green curry. Foreign travel and exotic holiday destinations have also made their mark on our culinary consciousness. European favourites include Italian pasta and pizza, Spanish paella, Greek baklava, French beef bourguignon and Bavarian Black Forest gâteau, while those who have ventured further afield voted for Japanese sushi, Mexican fajitas, Australian pavlova and Moroccan couscous.

This survey demonstrates that while we are loyal to our roots and relish old-fashioned home cooking, we have also become a nation of foodies with sophisticated palates and open minds, as well as open mouths. Undoubtedly, we could all argue endlessly about the final order of top dishes and some of the conclusions may well surprise. Indeed, the recipes with the top scores are not so predictable as you might think. Not long ago chicken tikka was said, somewhat controversially, to be Britain's national dish, so it's something of a shock to discover that the dish with the single highest vote is chicken satay. Perhaps more predictably, given our world-beating consumption of chocolate, second place of all goes to tiramisù. The overall favourite for light meals (after chicken satay) is English breakfast and the most popular main course is paella, beating roast beef by a mere 30 votes. Those with a sweet tooth who didn't vote for tiramisù chose cheesecake, closely followed by crème caramel.

What we like to eat and what we are willing or able to cook are not always quite the same thing. Lots of very popular restaurant dishes are extremely labour intensive, which is fine when you have a kitchen full of assistant chefs, but not such a good idea when there's just one or two of you trying to feed a hungry family after a hard day at work. Some mouthwatering delights depend, at least partially, on difficult-to-obtain or very expensive ingredients — fabulous for a celebration dinner but hardly appropriate for a midweek supper. And while enthusiastic amateur cooks can turn their hands to most things, few have the time to master all the techniques of the professional chef. So it seemed sensible that the recipes in this book should involve only skills and ingredients within the scope, time span available and everyday budgets of 'average' cooks, while still taking account of the differing requirements of throwing a dinner party and rustling up a quick snack. The recipes are designed to be easy to follow, even by inexperienced cooks or complete beginners, and the book is packed with extra hints and tips to make everything simpler and to guarantee success.

Of course, you can't fairly compare macaroni cheese, coq au vin and steak and chips, although they all had similar numbers of votes. Each is delicious in its own way and at the right time. That's why the recipes are divided into different categories, making it as easy as pie — or even a piece of cake — to choose a sure-fire favourite whenever friends are coming round.

> Many of my happiest childhood memories are to do with food: Christmas dinner, birthday teas, picnics on the beach and steaming stews when we got home from school.
>
> *Dave, Amersham*

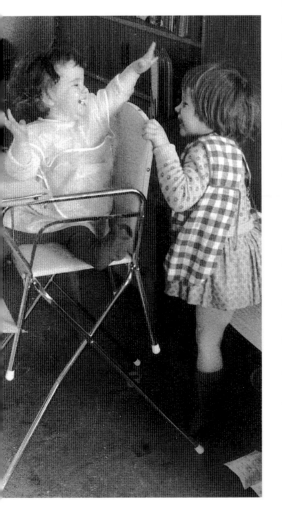

The way we ate

In some ways our eating habits have changed dramatically in the past 50 or so years. In others they have altered little and, what's more, some of the things we think of as changes simply aren't.

The years immediately following World War II were still a period of austerity — although gradually relaxed, rationing did not end completely until the early 1950s. Parents — and the government of the day — were eager to give children good food in sufficient quantities to provide healthy growth and plenty of energy. In spite of such treats as bread and butter pudding and apricot crumble, two long-lasting favourites which feature in this book, childhood obesity was virtually unheard of. Similarly, a low-fat diet was never considered; mums cooked with lard and dripping rather than monounsaturated and polyunsaturated oils. It's difficult to believe now that olive oil was mainly available from chemists rather than supermarkets.

Meat had always been expensive, so vegetables, potatoes, pastry and dumplings played important roles in satisfying appetites — baby boomers mostly ate their greens. The years of 'digging for victory' had ensured that

" Like listening to music, the smell and taste of food has the same effect of taking you back to a moment in time - vividly recapturing a memory. "

Lynne, London

indigenous vegetables and fruit, such as cabbages and carrots, apples and pears, were already an essential part of the family menu and with the re-establishment of international trade, imported produce such as oranges and bananas again became available.

The 1950s also witnessed the first large-scale, post-war immigration from the Caribbean but it was to be many years before such ingredients as sweet potatoes, plantains, okra and hot spices made their way on to mainstream supermarket shelves. In contrast, the hangover from colonial days continued to influence the British diet. Kedgeree and curries, which in a typical British adaptation tended to include sultanas and chunks of apple, had been appearing on British tables for at least 100 years.

The notorious insularity of Britain and the British encountered a major culture shock in the 1960s and 1970s. By this time, almost everyone owned a television, giving homes a window on the wider world; package tours offered affordable holidays in sunnier climes; people from an increasing number of countries set up homes and businesses, including restaurants, in our towns and cities; and a thriving economy combined with a powerful youth culture set the pace for change. While the wealthy had always been happy to patronize restaurants, they were a new discovery for those lower down the social scale as they encountered pasta in inexpensive Italian trattoria and chop suey – actually an invention of San Francisco's Chinatown – in the then rather exotic Chinese restaurants that seemed to spring up overnight.

Having experienced the flavours of Mediterranean cuisine during our holidays on the Costa Brava or in the South of France, we began to look for new ingredients in our shops – peppers, aubergines and pasta shapes, for example. A new style of cooking, different from 'meat and two veg', became fashionable. Of course, there were those who were horrified by 'made up' dishes, such as coq au vin, and whose aversion to garlic was surpassed only by Count Dracula's. Yet we have a British tradition of one-pot stews, although they tended not to include wine, and garlic features in English recipes that date from the Middle Ages.

Another cultural change began as the baby boomers grew up. In the past, it had been standard practice for grown-up children, particularly daughters, to remain in the parental home until they had married, set up their own homes and 'settled down'. However, the 'make love, not war' generation grasped their independence firmly in both hands and moved out into bedsits and often incredibly squalid flats, where they mastered the art of making 'spag bol' on inadequate gas rings. That, combined with a bottle of cheap Spanish plonk and a gathering of friends, was the height of decadence for many. As they moved on in life and up the property ladder, so their interest in food and their culinary skills developed – as well as their taste in wine.

It will be interesting to see if and how another social shift taking place currently affects our eating habits. Rocketing property prices and rents, as well as higher lifestyle expectations, have resulted in young adults flying the parental nest at a later age, with some returning even after they have done so. Parents who thought they were in for some quality me-time can now find themselves once more slaving over a hot stove trying to satisfy the appetites of their fully grown offspring.

The astonishing growth of take-away 'restaurants' and fast-food chains has also had an immense impact. Ordering pizza, curry or spring rolls on the phone or grabbing a burger on the run became a major convenience for stressed people with no time to cook and, of course, they still have a useful and popular place in modern life. However, this led to a second phase of development when food suppliers recognized a market for ready-made egg-fried rice or lamb rogan josh and began producing frozen and chilled versions, which started out as boil-in-the-bag, developed into oven-ready and, finally, could be zapped in the microwave in minutes. We are now witnessing a third phase where, because they are familiar with these once exotic dishes, people want to cook them themselves from fresh ingredients – hence many of the recipes that won votes in this book.

In the last two decades, the world has shrunk and we think nothing of flying to every continent and sampling the cuisines of countries as diverse as Japan, the United States, Mexico and Thailand. The popularity of gap years has encouraged us to stray off the beaten track to uncover the 'real' country and we have returned with a taste for foreign foods that have now become an intrinsic part of the British diet. Restaurants serving dishes from just about every culture, from Ethiopia to Iran, are commonplace and supermarkets are stocked with ingredients, from Thai fish sauce to North African couscous, that our mothers and grandmothers wouldn't recognize.

OUR FAVOURITE FOOD – HOW WE VOTED

Top Ten Recipes in Each Category

		% of vote in category
Light meals		
1	Chicken Satay	51.1
2	English Breakfast	40.7
3	Filled Jacket Potatoes (various)	37.1
4	Tortillas	32.6
5	Nachos	29.7
6	Crispy Potato Skins	28.5
7	Tapas	26.0
8	Salad (various)	24.4
9	Cauliflower Cheese	22.9
10	Spring Rolls	22.8
Main courses		
1	Paella	34.8
2	Roast Dinner (Beef/Turkey)	34.5
3	Moussaka/Vegetable Moussaka	28.7
4	Classic Fajitas	24.1
5	Spaghetti Bolognese	23.4
6	Chicken Cajun-Style	18.0
7	Lasagne Verde/Vegetable Lasagne	16.5
8	Stir-fry	15.0
9	Chilli con Carne/Vegetable Chilli	14.8
10	Calzone (various)	13.8
Desserts		
1	Tiramisù	41.6
2	Cheesecake (various)	37.1
3	Crème Caramel	35.5
4	Banoffee Pie	34.7
5	Carrot Cake	34.4
6	Fresh Fruit/Salad	28.7
7	Ice Cream	26.1
8	Profiteroles	24.9
9	Pecan Pie	24.1
10	Tarte Citron	21.8

Overall Top Ten Favourite Recipes

1	Chicken Satay	51.1
2	Tiramisù	41.6
3	English Breakfast	40.7
4	Filled Jacket Potatoes (various)	37.2
5	Cheesecake (various)	37.1
6	Crème Caramel	35.5
7	Paella	34.8
8	Banoffee Pie	34.7
9	Roast Dinner (Beef/Turkey)	34.5
10	Carrot Cake	34.4

Chapter one

LIKE MOTHER USED TO MAKE

The sizzling top vote in this chapter went to that unique speciality, English breakfast. The favourite main course is the classic roast beef of old England and crisp apple pie is the champion dessert.

light meals

Full English breakfast

An overall winner in this chapter, a 'proper' breakfast clearly hits the spot. Mum would approve too. It's great for the weekend when you not only have more time to cook it, but a real opportunity to relish every mouthful while perusing the newspapers.

SERVES 1

Preparation time: 10 minutes
Cooking time: 15–20 minutes

2 good-quality pork sausages

2–3 smoked back bacon rashers

2 eggs

vegetable oil

1 slice 2-day-old wholemeal bread (optional)

1 large tomato, halved

2–3 mushrooms

salt and pepper

1 Preheat the grill, then place the sausages under the hot grill and grill for 15–20 minutes, turning frequently, or until well browned.

2 Meanwhile, place the bacon rashers in a dry frying pan and fry for 2–4 minutes on each side, depending on how crisp you like your bacon. Remove them from the frying pan, leaving all the excess bacon fat, and keep the bacon warm. The frying pan can then be used to fry the eggs if you choose to have them fried (see page 16).

3 Add a little oil to the pan if necessary and then place the bread in the fat (if making). Cook for 1–2 minutes on one side, then turn over and repeat the process. Do not cook too quickly or the bread will burn.

4 Place the tomato halves under the hot grill with the sausages. Drizzle with a little oil and season to taste with salt and pepper before grilling for 3–4 minutes.

5 Either grill the mushrooms with the tomatoes or quickly fry them in the frying pan with a little extra oil added.

6 Arrange the sausages, bacon, eggs, fried bread, tomatoes and mushrooms on a large warmed plate and serve immediately.

"It has to be the most
effective hangover cure in
the whole world, even when
you haven't been drinking."

Chris, Barnsley

light meals

Cauliflower cheese 2

No wonder this is such a popular snack — it's quick and easy to make, inexpensive, packed with protein and vitamins, looks great and tastes wonderful. It's a sure-fire hit with kids and adults alike and a painless way to ensure everyone eats their vegetables.

SERVES 4

Preparation time: 10 minutes
Cooking time: 20 minutes

1 cauliflower, trimmed and cut
   into florets (675 g/1 lb 8 oz
   prepared weight)
40 g/1½ oz butter
40 g/1½ oz plain flour
450 ml/16 fl oz milk
115 g/4 oz Cheddar cheese,
   finely grated
whole nutmeg
1 tbsp freshly grated Parmesan
   cheese
salt and pepper

TO SERVE
1 small tomato
green salad
crusty bread

1 Cook the cauliflower in a saucepan of lightly salted boiling water for 4–5 minutes. It should still be firm. Drain, place in a hot 1.4-litre/2½-pint gratin dish and keep warm.

2 Melt the butter in the rinsed-out saucepan over a medium heat and stir in the flour. Cook for 1 minute, stirring constantly.

3 Remove from the heat and stir in the milk gradually until you have a smooth consistency.

4 Return to a low heat and continue to stir while the sauce comes to the boil and thickens. Reduce the heat and simmer gently, stirring constantly, for about 3 minutes, or until the sauce is creamy and smooth.

5 Remove the saucepan from the heat and stir in the Cheddar cheese and a good grating of the nutmeg. Season to taste with salt and pepper.

6 Preheat the grill. Pour the hot sauce over the cauliflower, top it with the Parmesan and place under the hot grill to brown. Serve immediately with a tomato, green salad and some crusty bread.

VARIATION
A mixture of broccoli and cauliflower florets makes a colourful and even more attractive dish. Meat eaters may also enjoy the addition of diced crispy bacon. Stir it in with the cheese in step 5.

" The best reward for doing my maths homework, even now a plateful of Cauliflower Cheese makes me feel I've been a good girl. "

Sally, Gloucester

light meals

Eggs

The iconic advertising slogan 'Go to work on an egg' still rings true. Quick, inexpensive, pretty much foolproof and totally yummy, an egg – however it is cooked – kick-starts the day at breakfast time or provides an almost instant snack whenever you're peckish.

Boiling

Preparation time: I minute
Cooking time: 3–10 minutes

You will need a saucepan large enough to cook the number of eggs required, but not so large that the eggs can move around too freely and crack. It is a good idea to ensure the eggs are at room temperature to prevent cracking. Fill the pan with water and heat to a simmer. Lower the eggs in with a long-handled spoon. Simmer for 3–4 minutes for soft-boiled, 5–6 for medium-boiled and 10 minutes for hard-boiled. If you are serving hard-boiled eggs cold, always run them under cold water immediately to prevent a black line forming around the yolk.

Poaching

Preparation time: I minute
Cooking time: 2–5 minutes

You need a small shallow pan (a small frying pan is ideal) and really fresh eggs for this particular method. Heat just enough water to cover the eggs and break I egg into a cup. When the water is at a gentle simmer, carefully pour in the egg and allow the white to coagulate around the yolk. Always cook poached eggs one at a time. Poach each egg for 2–3 minutes if you like a soft yolk or for 4–5 minutes for a firmer egg. Remove the poached eggs from the pan using a slotted spoon, then drain quickly on kitchen paper and serve immediately.

Frying

Preparation time: I minute
Cooking time: 3–4 minutes

The best way to fry an egg is in the frying pan in which you have just fried some bacon. This way you have some delicious bacon fat to baste your egg with. Otherwise, take I tablespoon oil and 15 g/½ oz butter and heat in a small frying pan over a medium heat. Break the egg into the frying pan (if you are a beginner it might be wise to break the egg into a cup or ramekin first). Fry the egg for a few seconds until the white sets, then baste with the fat to make sure it is evenly cooked, with the white completely set and the yolk still remaining soft in the centre. Remove the egg from the pan using a wooden spatula and allow it to rest on a piece of kitchen paper for a second to absorb any excess fat. Serve immediately.

Scrambling

Preparation time: 1 minute
Cooking time: 3–5 minutes

Allow 2 eggs per person and beat them lightly in a basin with a little salt and pepper. Melt 15 g/½ oz butter in a small saucepan over a low heat, pour in the beaten eggs and stir gently using a wooden spoon. The egg will start to set on the base of the pan, so lift it away from the base until all the egg is starting to look creamy. Remove from the heat and continue to stir until it does not look wet any more. Serve quickly as you do not want to have rubbery scrambled egg.

" There were six of us but my Mum always made sure we didn't leave for school without eating our eggs. I don't know how she managed. "

Sue, Scarborough

"We used to take this on picnics instead of boring old sandwiches. I think it made my Mum feel posh." *Diana, Reading*

light meals

Coronation chicken

4

Rather adventurous in its day, this summery favourite was created in 1953 to celebrate — what else — the coronation of Queen Elizabeth II in June of that year. A timeless classic, it has remained popular ever since. Don't forget that it makes ideal picnic food too.

SERVES 6

Preparation time: 10 minutes
Cooking time: 30 minutes
Cooling time: 1–1½ hours
Standing time: 1 hour

4 boneless chicken breasts

1 bay leaf

1 small onion, sliced

1 carrot, sliced

4 peppercorns

1 tbsp olive oil

2 shallots, finely chopped

2 tsp Indian curry paste

2 tsp tomato purée

juice of ½ lemon

300 ml/10 fl oz mayonnaise

150 ml/5 fl oz natural yogurt

85 g/3 oz ready-to-eat dried
  apricots, chopped

salt and pepper

2 tbsp chopped fresh parsley,
  to garnish

green salad, to serve

1 Place the chicken breasts in a large saucepan with the bay leaf, onion and carrot. Cover with water and add ½ teaspoon of salt and the peppercorns. Bring to the boil over a medium heat, reduce the heat and simmer very gently for 20–25 minutes. Remove the saucepan from the heat and leave the chicken to cool while still sitting in the liquid. Reserve 150 ml/5 fl oz of the stock for the sauce.

2 Meanwhile, heat the olive oil in a frying pan and sauté the shallots gently for 2–3 minutes until softened but not coloured. Stir in the curry paste and continue to cook for another minute. Stir in the reserved stock, the tomato purée and lemon juice and simmer for 10 minutes until the sauce is quite thick. Remove the pan from the heat and leave to cool.

3 Remove the chicken from the remaining stock, take off the skin and slice into neat pieces.

4 Mix the mayonnaise and yogurt together in a bowl, then stir the mixture into the sauce. Add the chopped apricots and season to taste with salt and pepper.

5 Stir the chicken into the sauce until well coated and then turn into a serving dish. Leave to stand for at least 1 hour for the flavours to mingle. Garnish with the chopped parsley and serve with a green salad.

COOK'S TIP

All kinds of curry pastes are available from supermarkets, but you can easily make a useful, all-purpose version at home. Grind together 2 dried red chillies, 2 curry leaves, 5 tbsp coriander seeds, 2 tbsp cumin seeds and 1 tbsp fenugreek seeds in a mortar with a pestle. Tip into a bowl and stir in 2 tsp curry powder, 1 tsp ground turmeric, 5 tbsp white wine vinegar and 2 tbsp water to make a paste. Heat 6 tbsp groundnut oil in a large, heavy-based frying pan. Add the curry paste and stir-fry over a medium–low heat for about 8 minutes until the oil rises to the surface. Leave to cool, then spoon into a clean, screw-top jar and store in the refrigerator.

light meals

Kedgeree

Dating from the days of the British Raj, this was once a favourite breakfast dish, but is now usually eaten for lunch or supper. The original Indian 'kadgeri' consisted of rice, onions, eggs and lentils; substituting smoked fish for the pulses was a British inspiration.

SERVES 4

Preparation time: 15 minutes
Cooking time: 30 minutes

450 g/1 lb undyed smoked
  haddock, skinned

2 tbsp olive oil

1 onion, finely chopped

1 tsp Indian curry paste

175 g/6 oz long-grain rice

55 g/2 oz butter

3 hard-boiled eggs

salt and pepper

2 tbsp chopped fresh parsley
  and a few sprigs, to garnish

1 Place the haddock in a large saucepan and cover with water. Bring the water to the boil, then turn down to a simmer and poach the fish for 8–10 minutes until it flakes easily.

2 Remove the fish and keep warm, reserving the water.

3 Heat the oil in a the saucepan and gently cook the onion for 4 minutes until softened. Stir in the curry paste and add the rice.

4 Measure 600 ml/1 pint of the haddock water and return this to the saucepan. Bring to a simmer and cover. Cook for 10–12 minutes until the rice is tender and the water has been absorbed. Season to taste with salt and pepper.

5 Flake the fish and add to the saucepan with the butter. Stir very gently over a low heat until the butter has melted. Chop 2 of the hard-boiled eggs and add these to the saucepan.

6 Transfer the kedgeree to a serving dish, slice the remaining egg and use it as a garnish. Scatter the parsley over and serve immediately, garnishing each person's plate with a parsley sprig.

VARIATION
Usually made with smoked haddock, Kedgeree can also be made with salmon and served as a lunch dish or at supper.

COOK'S TIP
Undyed smoked haddock is a pale creamy yellow colour rather than bright gold. As it's cold-smoked, the flesh should be moist and transparent. It has a better texture and a more delicious flavour than coloured smoked haddock but, inevitably, tends to be rather more expensive.

" We used to sit in the kitchen on a Sunday morning, waiting for breakfast as the smell of Kedgeree wafted through the house. "

Eliza, Wilton

" When I was travelling in India, I dreamed of Roast Beef and Yorkshire puddings. It's the first thing Mum cooked when I got back. "

John, Bristol

YORKSHIRE PUDDINGS

Make the batter as in step 3 on page 35 and leave to stand for 15–30 minutes. Meanwhile, spoon a little of the fat from the meat into 12 patty tins, or add a knob of lard or ½ tsp vegetable oil to each and place in a preheated oven 220°C/425°F/ Gas Mark 7. When the fat is hot, stir the batter and spoon it into the tins. Bake for 10–15 minutes, until risen and golden. Reduce the oven temperature to 190°C/375°F/Gas Mark 5 while you carve the beef, then serve immediately.

main courses

Roast dinner

The quintessential Sunday lunch, a prime piece of British beef, crisply coated roast potatoes with a melt-in-the-mouth centre and light-as-air Yorkshire pudding, all served with richly flavoured gravy, takes some beating. Understandably, this one ran away with the votes.

SERVES 8

Preparation time: 5 minutes
Cooking time: 2¼–2¾ hours
Standing time: 10–15 minutes

2.7 kg/6 lb prime rib of beef

2 tsp dry English mustard

3 tbsp plain flour

300 ml/10 fl oz red wine

300 ml/10 fl oz beef stock

2 tsp Worcestershire
  sauce (optional)

salt and pepper

TO SERVE

Yorkshire puddings

roast potatoes

freshly cooked vegetables

1 Preheat the oven to 230°C/450°F/Gas Mark 8.

2 Season the meat with salt and pepper and rub in the mustard and 1 tablespoon of flour.

3 Place the meat in a roasting tin large enough to hold it comfortably and roast it for 15 minutes. Then reduce the oven temperature to 190°C/375°F/Gas Mark 5 and cook for 15 minutes per 450 g/1 lb, plus 15 minutes (1 hour 45 minutes for this joint) for rare beef or 20 minutes per 450 g/1 lb, plus 20 minutes (2 hours 20 minutes) for medium beef. Baste the meat occasionally to keep it moist and if the tin becomes too dry, add a little of the red wine or stock to it.

4 Remove the meat from the oven and place on a hot serving plate, cover with foil and leave in a warm place for 10–15 minutes.

5 Pour off most of the fat from the roasting tin, leaving behind the meat juices and the sediment. Place the tin on the top of the hob over a medium heat and scrape all the sediments from the base of the tin. Sprinkle in the remaining flour and, using a small whisk, quickly mix it into the juices. When you have a smooth paste, gradually add the wine and most of the stock, whisking constantly. Bring to the boil, then turn down the heat to a gentle simmer and cook for 2–3 minutes. Season with salt and pepper and add the remaining stock, if needed, and a little Worcestershire sauce, if liked.

6 When ready to serve, carve the meat into slices and serve on warmed plates. Pour the gravy into a warmed jug and take direct to the table. Serve the roast beef with Yorkshire puddings, roast potatoes and freshly cooked vegetables.

main courses

Stew & dumplings

A classic winter warmer, this substantial, flavour-packed dish with its scrumptious herb dumplings, is the perfect way to keep out the cold. An easy-to-prepare, one-pot meal, it's perfect for family suppers or informal entertaining and will prove a winner with the cook too.

SERVES 6

Preparation time: 20 minutes
Cooking time: 2½–3 hours

3 tbsp olive oil

2 onions, finely sliced

2 garlic cloves, chopped

1 kg/2 lb 4 oz good-quality
    braising steak

2 tbsp plain flour

300 ml/10 fl oz beef stock

bouquet garni sachet
    (shop-bought)

150 ml/5 fl oz red wine

salt and pepper

1 tbsp chopped fresh parsley,
    to garnish

HERB DUMPLINGS

115 g/4 oz self-raising flour, plus
    extra for shaping

55 g/2 oz suet

1 tsp mustard

1 tbsp chopped fresh parsley

1 tsp chopped fresh sage

4 tbsp cold water

1 Preheat the oven to 150°C/300°F/Gas Mark 2.

2 Heat 1 tablespoon of the oil in a large frying pan, add the onions and garlic and fry until softened and browned. Remove from the frying pan using a slotted spoon and place in a large casserole.

3 Trim the meat and cut into thick strips. Using the remaining oil, fry the meat in the frying pan over a high heat, stirring well until it is browned all over.

4 Sprinkle in the flour and stir well to prevent lumps. Season well with salt and pepper.

5 Pour in the stock, stirring constantly to make a smooth sauce, then continue to heat over a medium heat until the sauce is boiling.

6 Transfer the contents of the frying pan to the casserole.

7 Add the bouquet garni and the wine. Cover and cook in the centre of the oven for 2–2½ hours.

8 Begin making the dumplings 20 minutes before the stew is ready. Place the dry ingredients in a bowl and mix well, then pour in enough of the water to form a firm but soft dough. Break the dough into 12 pieces and roll them into round dumplings (you might need some flour on your hands for this).

9 Remove the stew from the oven, check the seasoning, discard the bouquet garni and add the dumplings, pushing them down under the liquid. Cover and return the dish to the oven, continuing to cook for 15 minutes until the dumplings have doubled in size.

10 Serve the stew and dumplings piping hot with the parsley scattered over the top.

66 If I ever fell out with my boyfriend, my Mum would always cook it for me and it made me smile again. 99 *Natalie, Sleaford 20*

"Being one of four kids there was only usually one night a week when I had my favourite dinner – Shepherd's Pie on a Tuesday night made the journey home from school a happy one!" *Fiona, Manchester*

main courses

Shepherd's pie

With its decorative topping of fluffy mashed potato concealing a succulent combination of lamb mince, carrots and a rich sauce, this is a sure-fire hit with all the family. Don't forget its close cousin, cottage pie, made in the same way but using beef mince instead of lamb.

SERVES 8

Preparation time: 15 minutes
Cooking time: 1½ hours

1 tbsp olive oil

2 onions, finely chopped

2 garlic cloves, finely chopped

675 g/1 lb 8 oz good-quality
   fresh lamb mince

2 carrots, finely chopped

1 tbsp plain flour

225 ml/8 fl oz beef or chicken
   stock, plus extra if necessary

125 ml/4 fl oz red wine

Worcestershire sauce (optional)

salt and pepper

MASHED POTATO

675 g/1 lb 8 oz floury potatoes,
   such as King Edward,
   Maris Piper or Desirée, cut
   into chunks

55 g/2 oz butter

2 tbsp cream or milk

1 Preheat the oven to 180°C/350°F/Gas Mark 4.

2 Heat the oil in a large casserole and fry the onion until softened, then add the garlic and stir well.

3 Increase the heat and add the meat. Cook quickly to brown the meat all over, stirring constantly. Add the carrot and season well with salt and pepper.

4 Stir in the flour and add the stock and wine. Stir well and heat until simmering and thickened.

5 Cover the casserole and cook in the preheated oven for about 1 hour. Check the consistency occasionally and add a little more stock if required. The mixture should be quite thick but not dry. Season to taste with salt and pepper and add a little Worcestershire sauce, if desired.

6 While the meat is cooking, make the mashed potato. Cook the potatoes in a large saucepan of lightly salted boiling water for 15–20 minutes. Drain well and mash with a potato masher until smooth. Add the butter and cream and season well with salt and pepper.

7 Spoon the lamb mixture into an ovenproof serving dish and spread or pipe the potato on top.

8 Increase the oven temperature to 200°C/400°F/Gas Mark 6 and cook the pie for 15–20 minutes at the top of the oven until golden brown. You might like to finish it off under a medium-hot grill for a really crisp brown topping to the potato.

ACCOMPANIMENTS

Shepherd's pie is pretty much a meal in itself but green vegetables provide attractive colour and are also good for us. Stir-fried cabbage could prove a taste revelation. Cut out and discard the core from a small Savoy cabbage or half a medium one, then shred the leaves. Heat 2 tbsp vegetable oil in a preheated wok or heavy-based frying pan. Add the cabbage and stir-fry for 2 minutes. Transfer to a dish and toss with 1 tbsp lemon juice and 2 tsp caraway seeds.

main courses

Sausages & mash

4

Forget the image of bursting bangers and lumpy potato typical of the notorious 'greasy spoon' and loathsome school dinners of the past. For real home cooking, try this tasty take on tradition with crisp, golden sausages, parsley mash and onion gravy.

SERVES 4

Preparation time: 15 minutes
Cooking time: 40 minutes

8 good-quality sausages
1 tbsp oil

MASHED POTATO

900 g/2 lb floury potatoes, such
   as King Edward, Maris Piper
   or Desirée, cut into chunks
salt and pepper
55 g/2 oz butter
3 tbsp milk
2 tbsp chopped fresh parsley

ONION GRAVY

3 onions, cut in half and
   thinly sliced
70 g/2½ oz butter
125 ml/4 fl oz Marsala or port
125 ml/4 fl oz vegetable stock
salt and pepper

1 Cook the sausages slowly in a frying pan with the oil over a low heat. Cover the pan and turn the sausages occasionally. Don't rush them because you want them well cooked and sticky. They will take 25–30 minutes.

2 Meanwhile, to make the mashed potato, cook the potatoes in a large saucepan of lightly salted boiling water for 15–20 minutes. Drain well and mash with a potato masher until smooth. Season with salt and pepper, add the butter, milk and parsley and stir well.

3 Prepare the onion gravy by placing the onions in a frying pan with the butter and frying over a low heat until soft, stirring constantly. Continue to cook until the onions are a good brown colour and are almost melting, stirring them occasionally. This process will take 30 minutes, but it is worth it as the onions will naturally caramelize.

4 Pour in the Marsala and stock and continue to bubble away until the onion gravy is really thick. Season to taste with salt and pepper.

5 Place the mashed potato in individual dishes and place the sausages on top, then spoon the onion gravy over them.

"The mash piled up like a mountain (just like in 'Close Encounters of the Third Kind'), then the sausages strategically stuffed into the mash like horns." *Mark, Doncaster*

" Reminds me of my childhood when
it was served as a rare treat. **"**

Margaret, Milton Keynes

main courses

Steak & kidney pudding

5

A rich and hearty dish that is always popular with meat-lovers, this is made with suet crust pastry. A British invention, this pastry has a wonderfully light spongy texture and turns golden brown on top. The contrasting textures of filling and pastry, plus the yummy gravy, make this a champion.

SERVES 4

Preparation time: 25 minutes
Cooking time: 4–5 hours

butter, for greasing

450 g/1 lb braising steak

3 lamb's kidneys

55 g/2 oz flour

1 onion, finely chopped

115 g/4 oz large field
  mushrooms, sliced (optional)

1 tbsp chopped fresh parsley

300 ml/10 fl oz stock or a
  mixture of beer and water

salt and pepper

SUET PASTRY

350 g/12 oz self-raising flour

175 g/6 oz suet

225 ml/8 fl oz cold water

1 Grease a 1.2-litre/2-pint pudding basin.

2 Trim the meat and cut into 2.5-cm/1-inch pieces. Cut the kidneys in half, remove the cores and cut into similar-sized pieces.

3 Place the prepared meat with the flour and some salt and pepper in a polythene bag and shake until all the meat is well floured. Add the onion, mushrooms, if using, and the parsley and shake again. Reserve.

4 Make the suet pastry by mixing the flour, suet and some salt and pepper together. Add enough of the cold water to make a soft dough.

5 Keep a quarter of the dough to one side and roll the remainder out to form a round large enough to line the pudding basin. As you line the basin, make sure that there is a good 1 cm/½ inch overlap.

6 Place the meat mixture in the basin and pour in enough of the stock to cover the meat.

7 Roll out the remaining pastry to make a lid. Dampen the edges and place the lid on top, folding any overlapping pastry. Seal the lid firmly in place.

8 Cover the pudding with a double sheet of foil, pleated in the centre to allow room for expansion while cooking. Secure it with string, making a handle so that you can lift it out of the steamer. Place it in a steamer or large saucepan half-filled with boiling water. Simmer the pudding for 4–5 hours, topping up the water occasionally.

9 Remove the basin from the steamer and take off the coverings. Wrap a clean cloth around the basin and serve at the table.

ACCOMPANIMENTS

The traditional vegetables to serve with steak and kidney pudding are mashed potatoes and green beans or peas. As it's a winter dish, peas will probably be frozen, so liven up the flavour with some extra ingredients. Shred 6 Cos lettuce leaves – the outer coarse leaves are ideal. Melt 25 g/1 oz butter in a saucepan and add the lettuce and 1 sliced shallot. Cook over a medium heat, stirring, for 5 minutes. Add 225 g/8 oz frozen peas and season with salt, pepper and a pinch of nutmeg. Stir well, cover, reduce the heat and cook for 5 minutes.

main courses

Lamb 6 cutlets

The sweet flavour and melting tenderness of spring lamb are perfectly partnered with the intense aroma of fresh rosemary and the sharpness of lemon juice in this simple but irresistible classic dish. It's great for a barbecue and works equally well grilled in the kitchen.

SERVES 4

Preparation time: 10 minutes
Marinating time: 1 hour
Cooking time: 10–15 minutes

8 lamb cutlets

5 tbsp olive oil

2 tbsp lemon juice

1 garlic clove, crushed

½ tsp lemon pepper

8 fresh rosemary sprigs

salt

jacket potatoes, to serve

SALAD

4 tomatoes, sliced

**4 spring onions, sliced
   diagonally**

DRESSING

2 tbsp olive oil

1 tbsp lemon juice

1 garlic clove, chopped

**¼ tsp finely chopped
   fresh rosemary**

1 Trim the lamb cutlets by cutting away the flesh with a sharp knife to expose the tips of the bones.

2 Place the oil, lemon juice, garlic, lemon pepper and salt into a shallow, non-metallic dish and whisk with a fork to combine.

3 Lay the rosemary sprigs in the dish and place the lamb on top. Leave to marinate for at least 1 hour, turning the lamb cutlets once.

4 Remove the cutlets from the marinade and wrap a little foil around the bones to stop them from burning.

5 Preheat the barbecue or grill. Place the rosemary sprigs on a barbecue rack or grill and place the lamb on top. Barbecue or grill for 10–15 minutes, turning once.

6 Meanwhile make the salad and dressing. Arrange the tomatoes on a serving dish and scatter the spring onions on top. Place all the ingredients for the dressing in a screw-top jar, shake well and pour over the salad. Serve with the lamb cutlets and jacket potatoes.

COOK'S TIP

For a more pronounced herb flavour, use rosemary vinegar in the dressing instead of the lemon juice and fresh rosemary. To make the herb vinegar, place as many fresh rosemary sprigs as possible in a sterilized preserving jar and then fill up with white wine vinegar. Seal the jar and place it in a sunny position for 4 weeks. Strain the vinegar through a very fine sieve or muslin into a small saucepan. Heat gently to just below boiling point. Leave to cool, then pour into a clean, dry bottle. Add 1–2 fresh rosemary sprigs, seal and store in a cool dark place for up to 6 months.

" My Mum used to serve these with those little paper frills on the ends when we had guests for dinner. I thought that was very refined. "

Caroline, Nottingham

main courses

Toad in the hole

In spite of its humorous name, this combination of sausages baked in crisp, golden batter is no joke. (You only get real toads if your mother's name is Morticia Addams.) Economical, tasty and filling, it makes a great family supper in the middle of the week.

SERVES 4

Preparation time: 10 minutes
Standing time: 30 minutes
Cooking time: 45–55 minutes

butter, for greasing

115 g/4 oz plain flour

pinch of salt

1 egg, beaten

300 ml/10 fl oz milk

450 g/1 lb good-quality sausages

1 tbsp vegetable oil

1 Preheat the oven to 220°C/425°F/Gas Mark 7.

2 Grease a 20 × 25-cm/ 8 ×10-inch ovenproof dish or roasting tin.

3 Make the batter by sifting the flour and salt into a large bowl. Make a well in the centre and add the beaten egg and half the milk. Carefully mix the liquid into the flour until the mixture is smooth. Gradually beat in the remaining milk. Leave to stand for 30 minutes.

4 Prick the sausages and place them in the ovenproof dish. Sprinkle over the oil and cook the sausages in the oven for 10 minutes until they are beginning to colour and the fat has begun to run and is sizzling.

5 Remove from the oven and quickly pour the batter over the sausages. Return to the oven and cook for 35–45 minutes, or until the toad is well risen and golden brown. Serve immediately.

VARIATION

For extra flavour, cut the sausages in half lengthways and spread the cut surfaces with hot English mustard or milder Dijon. Sandwich them back together before placing them in the dish and cooking in the oven.

" By far my favourite dish — it brings back memories of coming home from school to a lovely smell — and a hearty meal! "

Heidi, Norwich

main courses

Macaroni cheese

8

This has been a family favourite since the nineteenth century — Mrs Beeton included three different ways to prepare it in her Book of Household Management. This up-to-date and rather more convenient version would undoubtedly have got her vote.

SERVES 4

Preparation time: 25 minutes
Cooking time: 45–50 minutes

600 ml/1 pint béchamel sauce (see page 114)

225 g/8 oz macaroni

1 egg, beaten

125 g/4½ oz mature Cheddar cheese, grated

1 tbsp wholegrain mustard

2 tbsp chopped fresh chives

4 tomatoes, sliced

125 g/4½ oz Red Leicester cheese, grated

60 g/2¼ oz blue cheese, grated

2 tbsp sunflower seeds

salt and pepper

snipped fresh chives, to garnish

COOK'S TIP

When you're cooking for children — especially if they're fussy eaters — bake and serve the macaroni cheese in individual ovenproof dishes. You'll need to reduce the cooking time by about 10 minutes.

1 Preheat the oven to 190°C/375°F/Gas Mark 5.

2 Make the béchamel sauce, place in a bowl and cover with clingfilm to prevent a skin forming.

3 Bring a saucepan of lightly salted water to the boil and cook the macaroni for 8–10 minutes, or until just tender. Drain well and place in an ovenproof dish.

4 Stir the beaten egg, Cheddar cheese, mustard, chives and seasoning into the béchamel sauce. Spoon the mixture over the macaroni, making sure it is well covered. Top with a layer of the sliced tomatoes.

5 Sprinkle the Red Leicester and blue cheeses, and sunflower seeds over the top. Place on a baking tray and bake for 25–30 minutes, or until the dish is bubbling and golden. Garnish with snipped fresh chives and serve immediately.

"The only thing I'd eat as a kid — now I'd eat anything, but no one makes Macaroni Cheese like my Mum." *Hazel, Creetown*

"My best mate always had tea at my house on a Friday when my Mum made Fish Pie. He's still my best mate and Fish Pie's still our favourite.**"** *Brian, Leeds*

main courses

Fish pie

In spite of the recommendations of nutritionists and our living in a country surrounded by sea, we eat surprisingly little fish, but this creamy, potato-topped pie is a perennial favourite loved by adults and children alike. For piscine perfection, make sure you remove all the pin bones.

SERVES 4

Preparation time: 15 minutes
Cooking time: 1¼ hours

350 g/12 oz haddock fillets

350 g/12 oz halibut fillets

350 g/12 oz salmon fillets

600 ml/1 pint milk

125 ml/4 fl oz brandy

1 kg/2 lb 4 oz floury potatoes
  such as King Edward or Maris
  Piper, sliced

5 tbsp butter, plus extra
  for greasing

3 tbsp plain flour

1 tbsp chopped fresh parsley

1 tbsp chopped fresh coriander

2 onions, 1 grated and 1 sliced

75 g/2¾ oz Cheddar cheese,
  grated

salt and pepper

cooked vegetables, to serve

1 Preheat the oven to 200°C/400°F/Gas Mark 6.

2 Rinse all the fish, then pat dry with kitchen paper. Pour the milk into a frying pan and bring to the boil. Add the haddock and halibut and cook for 10 minutes. Lift out and set aside. Reserve the milk. In another pan, cook the salmon in the brandy over a low heat for 10 minutes. Lift out and set aside. Reserve the liquid. Cut all the fish into small chunks.

3 Cook the potatoes in a saucepan of lightly salted boiling water for 15 minutes. Meanwhile, melt the butter in another pan over a low heat, stir in the flour and cook for 1 minute. Stir in the reserved milk and brandy liquid to make a smooth sauce. Bring to the boil, then simmer for 10 minutes. Remove from the heat and stir in the herbs.

4 Drain and mash the potatoes, then add the grated onion. Season. Grease a large pie dish with butter, then add the fish. Top with the sliced onion. Pour over enough sauce to cover. Top with potato, then grated cheese. Bake for 30 minutes. Serve with cooked vegetables.

COOK'S TIP

Although the main bones will all have been removed from fish fillets, tiny bones, known as pin bones, may remain. These will spoil the texture of the pie, can be unpleasant if swallowed and are likely to put children off fish for life. Before cooking the fish, remove as many of these bones as you can – pulling them out with tweezers is often the easiest way. Also, keep an eye open for any remaining bones when you are cutting the fish into chunks at the end of step 2.

main courses

Bubble & squeak

Originally created to use up leftover vegetables — and occasionally the meat — from the Sunday roast, bubble and squeak is now a popular dish in its own right. Its unusual name comes from the sounds the vegetables make when they are boiled in water and then fried in hot fat.

SERVES 4

Preparation time: 20 minutes
Cooking time: 1 hour

450 g/1 lb floury potatoes,
   peeled and diced

2 tbsp milk

55 g/2 oz butter

salt and pepper

225 g/8 oz green cabbage,
   shredded

225 g/8 oz carrots, sliced thinly

1 medium onion, chopped

55 g/2 oz Cheddar cheese,
   grated

1 Cook the potatoes in salted water for 10 minutes, or until soft. Drain well and turn into a large mixing bowl. Mash until smooth. Beat with the milk, half of the butter and salt and pepper to taste.

2 Cook the cabbage and carrots separately in salted boiling water for 5 minutes. Drain well. Mix the cabbage into the potatoes.

3 Melt the remaining butter in a small frying pan and cook the onion over a medium heat until soft but not brown.

4 Preheat the oven to 190°C/375°F/Gas Mark 5. Spread a layer of mashed potatoes in the bottom of a greased shallow ovenproof dish. Layer onions on top, then carrots. Repeat to use up all the ingredients, finishing with a layer of potato.

5 Sprinkle the grated cheese on top, place the dish in the oven and bake for 45 minutes, or until the top is golden and crusty. Remove from the oven and serve immediately.

VARIATION

Try using Brussels sprouts instead of cabbage. Cook in lightly salted boiling water for 3–5 minutes. Drain, chop and add to the potato in Step 2.

"Bubble and Squeak on a Monday night... always! How Mum always had enough Sunday veg left over to feed seven of us the following day I'll never know!" *Denise, Basingstoke*

"New things come and go but Apple Pie and custard will always take some beating!

Kirsty, Bolton

desserts

Apple pie

Apples have long been the most popular fruit in Britain and now many specialist growers are reviving old-fashioned varieties. Whatever apples you use, they are rarely more delicious than when cooked in a crisp pastry base with lemon and spices, served with cream or custard.

SERVES 4

Preparation time: 25 minutes
Resting time: 30 minutes
Cooking time: 35 minutes

PASTRY

200 g/7 oz plain flour, plus extra
   for dusting

100 g/3½ oz butter, diced, plus
   extra for greasing

50 g/1¾ oz icing sugar, sifted

finely grated rind of 1 lemon

1 egg yolk, beaten

3 tbsp milk

FILLING

3 cooking apples

2 tbsp lemon juice

finely grated rind of 1 lemon

150 ml/5 fl oz clear honey

175 g/6 oz fresh white or
   wholemeal breadcrumbs

1 tsp ground mixed spice

pinch of freshly grated nutmeg

whipped cream, to serve

1 To make the pastry, sift the flour into a bowl, then rub in the butter. Mix in the icing sugar, lemon rind, egg yolk and milk. Knead briefly on a lightly floured work surface, then leave to rest for 30 minutes.

2 Preheat the oven to 200°C/400°F/Gas Mark 6. Grease a 20-cm/8-inch flan tin with butter. Roll out the pastry to a thickness of 5 mm/¼ inch and use it to line the base and sides of the tin.

3 To make the filling, core 2 cooking apples and grate them into a bowl. Add 1 tablespoon of the lemon juice and all the lemon rind, along with the honey, breadcrumbs and mixed spice. Mix together well, then spoon evenly into the pastry case.

4 Core and slice the remaining apple, and use to decorate the top of the pie. Brush the apple slices with the remaining lemon juice, then sprinkle over the nutmeg. Bake the pie in the preheated oven for 35 minutes, or until it is firm. Remove from the oven and serve with whipped cream.

ACCOMPANIMENTS

Instead of whipped cream, serve this pie with home-made custard. Pour 500 ml/18 fl oz milk into a saucepan and add a split vanilla pod. Bring to just below boiling point, then remove from the heat and reserve. Whisk together 8 egg yolks and 250 g/9 oz caster sugar in a bowl until pale and thickened. Remove the vanilla pod from the milk and gradually stir the milk into the egg mixture. Pour the mixture into the saucepan and heat gently, stirring constantly. When the custard has thickened enough to cling to a spoon – just before it comes to the boil – strain it into a jug. If you're not ready to serve immediately, strain the custard into a bowl and keep warm over a saucepan of barely simmering water. If you place a round of greaseproof paper on the surface, it will not form a skin.

desserts

Fruit crumble 2

Some clever cook who was short of time must have invented this tempting alternative to a fruit pie. Softened, sweet fruit and a crisp, golden topping provide the perfect combination of textures. It tastes great served hot, warm or cold — on its own or with cream.

SERVES 4

Preparation time: 15 minutes
Cooking time: 35 minutes

125 g/4½ oz butter, plus extra
  for greasing
175 g/6 oz brown sugar
500 g/1 lb 2 oz fresh apricots,
  stoned and sliced
1 tsp ground cinnamon
175 g/6 oz wholemeal flour
50 g/1¾ oz toasted and finely
  chopped hazelnuts
clotted cream, to serve

1 Preheat the oven to 200°C/400°F/Gas Mark 6. Grease a 1.2-litre/2-pint ovenproof dish with butter.

2 Place 3 tablespoons of the butter and 100 g/3½ oz of the sugar in a saucepan and melt, stirring, over a low heat. Add the apricots and cinnamon, cover and simmer for 5 minutes.

3 Meanwhile, make the crumble topping. Place the flour in a bowl and rub in the remaining butter. Stir in the remaining sugar, then the hazelnuts.

4 Remove the fruit from the heat and arrange in the base of the prepared dish. Sprinkle the crumble topping evenly over the fruit until it is covered all over.

5 Transfer the dish to the preheated oven and bake for 25 minutes until golden. Remove from the oven and serve hot with clotted cream on top.

" We used to call this 'wait and see' because that's what my Mum always said when we sniffed the air and asked 'what's for pudding?'. "

Mike, Liverpool

desserts

Bread & butter pudding

Once a 'waste not, want not' way of using up stale bread and making an inexpensive family dessert, this modest dish has now been elevated to the ranks of gourmet cooking by at least one of our leading chefs. You can vary the dried fruit depending on what you like best.

SERVES 4

Preparation time: 15 minutes
Cooking time: 40 minutes

6 slices of day-old wholemeal
  bread, crusts removed

2 tbsp butter, plus extra for
  greasing

2 tbsp sugar

25 g/1 oz sultanas

25 g/1 oz currants

425 ml/15 fl oz milk

2 eggs

½ tsp ground mixed spice

1 Preheat the oven to 180°C/350°F/Gas Mark 4. Spread the slices of bread with butter, then cut each slice into quarters. Grease an 850-ml/1½-pint ovenproof dish, then arrange half of the bread, buttered side up, on the base of the dish.

2 Sprinkle over half of the sugar, then scatter over half of the sultanas and currants. Top this with the remaining bread and then sprinkle over the remaining sugar and fruit.

3 Pour the milk into a large mixing bowl. Add the eggs and mixed spice and whisk until smooth. Pour the mixture evenly over the bread, then transfer to the preheated oven and bake for 40 minutes. Remove from the oven and serve hot.

" For years I thought it was a joke. I didn't believe that you could make something this good from something that simple. "

Jenny, Colwyn Bay

desserts

Lemon meringue pie

A sweet, tangy filling and a melt-in-the-mouth topping contrast superbly with a crisp pastry shell. This ever-popular dessert looks every bit as lovely as it tastes. It's usually served hot and there's rarely any left over, but, if there is, it's also good cold the next day.

SERVES 4

Preparation time: 25 minutes
Resting time: 30 minutes
Cooking time: 1 hour

PASTRY

200 g/7 oz plain flour, plus extra for dusting

100 g/3½ oz butter, diced, plus extra for greasing

50 g/1¾ oz icing sugar, sifted

finely grated rind of 1 lemon

1 egg yolk, beaten

3 tbsp milk

FILLING

3 tbsp cornflour

300 ml/10 fl oz cold water

juice and grated rind of 2 lemons

175 g/6 oz caster sugar

2 eggs, separated

1 To make the pastry, sift the flour into a large bowl and rub in the butter. Then mix in the remaining ingredients. Knead briefly on a lightly floured work surface. Leave to rest for 30 minutes.

2 Preheat the oven to 180°C/350°F/Gas Mark 4. Grease a 20-cm/8-inch ovenproof flan dish with butter.

3 Roll out the pastry to a thickness of 5 mm/¼ inch and line the dish with it. Prick with a fork, then line with greaseproof paper and fill with baking beans. Bake for 15 minutes. Remove from the oven, then reduce the oven temperature to 150°C/300°F/Gas Mark 2.

4 To make the filling, mix the cornflour with a little water to make a paste. Pour the remaining water into a saucepan. Stir in the lemon juice and rind and cornflour paste. Bring to the boil, while stirring, and cook for 2 minutes. Cool slightly, then stir in 5 tablespoons of the sugar and the egg yolks and pour into the pastry case. In a separate bowl, whisk the egg whites until stiff. Gradually whisk in the remaining sugar and spread over the pie. Bake in the oven for 40 minutes, until the meringue is light brown. Remove from the oven and serve.

COOK'S TIP

Partially baking the pastry case, called 'baking blind', prevents a moist filling from seeping through during cooking. You can use baking paper, greaseproof paper or foil. Cut out a round that will fit the base of the case, put it in position and then weigh it down with baking beans. These may be real beans, such as dried butter beans, which you should keep just for this purpose as they will be completely inedible. Otherwise, you can buy aluminium beans from kitchen shops. Spread a thick, even layer over the base and tight against the sides. Their weight will prevent the pastry case from shrinking and blistering during the initial baking. The beans are easily removed with the lining.

"My Mum would always bake me a Lemon Meringue Pie for my birthday — she still does whenever I visit." *Sue, Ely*

desserts

Trifle

A trifle means a thing of little value, but in spite of its name, this dish is not something to dismiss lightly. Known in Ireland as tipsy cake and in Scotland as whim-wham, recipes for this attractive – and alcoholic – fruit-filled dessert date back to the sixteenth century.

SERVES 4

Preparation time: 20 minutes
Cooling time: 30 minutes
Cooking time: 10 minutes
Chilling time: 4 hours

FRUIT LAYER

6 trifle sponge cakes

2 tbsp strawberry jam

6 large strawberries, hulled and sliced

2 bananas, peeled and sliced

400 g/14 oz canned sliced peaches, drained

6 tbsp sherry

CUSTARD LAYER

250 ml/9 fl oz double cream

1 tsp vanilla essence

3 egg yolks

4 tbsp caster sugar

TOPPING

300 ml/10 fl oz double cream

2 tbsp caster sugar

chopped mixed nuts, toasted, to decorate

1 To make the fruit layer, spread the sponge cakes with jam, cut into bite-sized pieces and arrange in the base of a glass serving bowl. Scatter over the fruit, pour over the sherry and reserve.

2 To make the custard, place the cream and vanilla essence in a saucepan and bring almost to the boil over a low heat. Meanwhile, place the egg yolks and sugar in a pudding basin and whisk together. Remove the cream mixture from the heat and gradually stir into the egg mixture. Return the mixture to the saucepan and warm over a low heat, stirring, until thickened. Remove the custard from the heat and leave to cool for 30 minutes, then pour it over the fruit layer. Cover with clingfilm and chill for 2½ hours.

3 Remove the trifle from the refrigerator. To make the topping, whip the cream and sugar together, then spread it evenly over the custard layer. Scatter the toasted, chopped mixed nuts over the top, then cover again with clingfilm and chill for a further 1½ hours. Serve chilled.

VARIATION

If you are making this trifle for children, you can substitute orange juice for the sherry, and hundreds and thousands for the chopped nuts.

COOK'S TIP

Individual trifles look pretty. Use sundae glasses or large wine goblets and divide the ingredients equally between them.

"When my auntie, uncle and cousins came to Sunday tea, serving the trifle was a ritual we looked forward to all day, if not all week." *Pete, Middlesborough*

desserts

Sticky toffee pudding

This classic dessert, hailing from the Lake District but popular throughout the country, is great comfort food for a cold winter evening or lunch on a wet weekend. This date-filled pudding is packed with chopped dates and covered with a wonderfully indulgent toffee sauce.

SERVES 4

Preparation time: 10–15 minutes
Cooking time: 35–40 minutes

PUDDING

75 g/2¾ oz sultanas

150 g/5½ oz stoned dates, chopped

1 tsp bicarbonate of soda

2 tbsp butter, plus extra for greasing

200 g/7 oz brown sugar

2 eggs

200 g/7 oz self-raising flour, sifted

STICKY TOFFEE SAUCE

2 tbsp butter

175 ml/6 fl oz double cream

200 g/7 oz brown sugar

zested orange rind, to decorate

freshly whipped cream, to serve

1 To make the pudding, put the fruits and bicarbonate of soda into a heatproof bowl. Cover with boiling water and leave to soak.

2 Preheat the oven to 180°C/ 350°F/Gas Mark 4. Grease a round cake tin, 20 cm/8 inches in diameter, with butter.

3 Put the remaining butter in a separate bowl, add the sugar and mix well. Beat in the eggs then fold in the flour. Drain the soaked fruits, add to the bowl and mix. Spoon the mixture evenly into the prepared cake tin. Transfer to the preheated oven and bake for 35–40 minutes. The pudding is cooked when a skewer inserted into the centre comes out clean.

4 About 5 minutes before the end of the cooking time, make the sauce. Melt the butter in a saucepan over a medium heat. Stir in the cream and sugar and bring to the boil, stirring constantly. Lower the heat and simmer for 5 minutes.

5 Turn out the pudding onto a serving plate and pour over the sauce. Decorate with zested orange rind and serve with whipped cream.

" We had sticky toffee pudding as our wedding breakfast dessert. Everyone loved it – they said how different it was and how it made a change from profiteroles! *Katherine, Surbiton*

"It's the simple
things that are
still absolutely
delicious, like hot
toast and butter."
Jennie, St. Minver

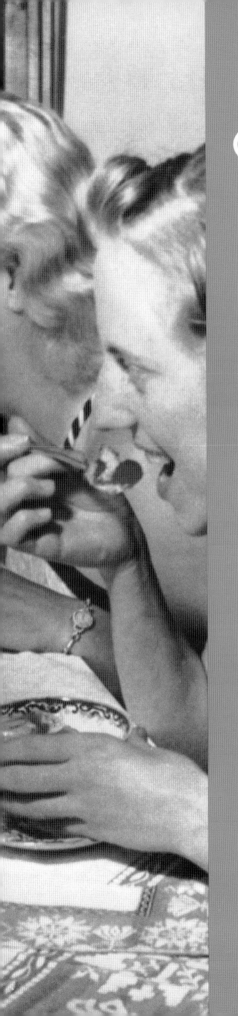

Chapter two

DINNER PARTY DAZZLERS

Top of the list for light meals are crispy potato skins. For a main course, lamb shanks are fashionable in the trendiest restaurants and scored the highest marks for dinner parties. A profusion of profiteroles was voted the most popular dessert.

light meals

Crispy potato skins

Fun finger food, this is the perfect choice for breaking the ice and getting the evening — and the meal — off to a great start. Filled with a mouthwatering mixture of crisp bacon and creamy blue cheese, they're easy to cook, so you're free to concentrate on the main course.

SERVES 4

Preparation time: 10 minutes
Cooking time: 10 minutes, plus 45–60 minutes for cooking the potatoes

4 potatoes, cooked in
  their skins
2 streaky bacon rashers
115 g/4 oz blue cheese,
  crumbled
vegetable oil, for deep-frying

TO GARNISH
crème fraîche or soured cream
snipped fresh chives

1 Cut the cooked potatoes in half and scoop out the soft inside, leaving a lining that is about 5 mm/¼ inch thick.

2 Grill the bacon until crisp. Transfer to a plate and cut into small strips. Combine the blue cheese and bacon in a small mixing bowl.

3 Heat the oil over a high heat in a wok or deep saucepan. Carefully drop the potato skins into the oil and deep-fry for 3–4 minutes, or until crisp and golden. Remove and drain well on kitchen paper.

4 Arrange the potato skins on a large plate and fill each with spoonfuls of the bacon and cheese mixture, piling it so high that it is almost overflowing. Garnish with a teaspoon of crème fraîche or soured cream, sprinkle some snipped fresh chives on top and serve immediately.

ACCOMPANIMENTS
You could also serve these filled potato skins with Guacamole (see page 189) or this delicious mustard mayonnaise. Put 2 egg yolks, 3 roughly chopped garlic cloves and 2 tbsp lemon juice in a blender or food processor and process briefly until smooth. With the motor running, gradually add 150 ml/5 fl oz olive oil and 150 ml/5 fl oz sunflower oil until the mixture has the consistency of mayonnaise. Scrape into a bowl, stir in 1 tbsp wholegrain mustard and season to taste with salt and pepper.

“ Prawn cocktail, coq au vin and Black Forest gâteau: my first ever dinner party menu — very 1980s! ”

Tracey, Nottingham

light meals

Prawn cocktail 2

Like the little girl in the nursery rhyme, this is one of those dishes that when it's good — and it is here — it's very, very good, but when it's bad, it's horrid. Succulent fresh prawns packed with flavour, crisp lettuce and a creamy dressing that's not too sharp are the secrets of success.

SERVES 4

Preparation time: 20 minutes

1 avocado

1 tbsp lemon juice

500 g/1 lb 2 oz cooked peeled
  prawns

crisp lettuce leaves

DRESSING

1 egg

2 tsp sherry vinegar

½ tsp mustard

dash of Worcestershire sauce

pinch of salt

300 ml/10 fl oz sunflower oil

100 ml/3½ fl oz tomato
  ketchup

TO GARNISH

pinch of paprika

strips of lemon zest

4 whole cooked prawns
  (optional)

1 To make the dressing, break the egg into a food processor. Add the vinegar, mustard, Worcestershire sauce and salt and process for 15 seconds. With the motor still running, gradually pour the oil through the feeder tube until thoroughly incorporated. Transfer the dressing to a large bowl, then stir in the tomato ketchup. Cover with clingfilm and leave to chill in the refrigerator until required.

2 Cut the avocado in half lengthways, then remove and discard the stone and skin. Cut the flesh into slices, then brush the flesh with lemon juice in order to prevent any discolouring.

3 To assemble the salad, take the dressing from the refrigerator, add the avocado and prawns and stir gently until coated.

4 Divide the lettuce leaves between large individual serving glasses or bowls. Fill each one with prawns, then garnish with paprika and lemon zest strips. If using whole prawns, hang a whole cooked prawn on the rim of each glass or bowl. Serve immediately.

COOK'S TIP

There is a huge variety of prawns available, varying in length from 5–18 cm/2–7 inches. Although usually quite small, cold-water prawns from the North Atlantic have an excellent flavour, while the large tiger prawns from the Pacific may sometimes look more spectacular than they taste. Mediterranean prawns, also known as king prawns, are medium-sized and have a fine flavour. Frozen cooked prawns don't have much flavour and their texture tends to be quite soggy, so they are better avoided for this dish. If you have to buy frozen prawns, buy raw ones, thaw completely, then shallow-fry in olive oil or griddle for a few minutes until they have turned pink and are cooked through. Leave to cool before making the cocktail.

light meals

Bruschetta with tomatoes

Like all the best Italian dishes, this couldn't be simpler but its flavour depends on using high-quality, though not necessarily expensive, ingredients. Follow that rule and these colourful, tomato-topped toasts are a lovely way to get the taste buds tingling.

SERVES 4

Preparation time: 10 minutes
Marinating time: 5 minutes
Cooking time: 5 minutes

125 ml/4 fl oz extra virgin
   olive oil
I small oval-shaped loaf of
   white bread (ciabatta or bloomer),
   cut into 1-cm/½-inch slices
4 tomatoes, deseeded and
   diced
6 fresh basil leaves, torn, plus
   whole leaves, to garnish
8 black olives, stoned and
   chopped
I large garlic clove, halved
salt and pepper
4 tomato roses, to garnish

1 Pour half of the oil into a shallow dish and place the bread in it. Leave for 1–2 minutes, then turn and leave for a further 2 minutes. The bread should be thoroughly saturated in oil.

2 Meanwhile, place the tomatoes in a mixing bowl. Sprinkle the basil leaves over the tomatoes. Season to taste with salt and pepper. Add the olives. Pour over the remaining olive oil. Leave to marinate while you toast the bruschetta.

3 Preheat the grill to medium. Place the bread on the grill rack and cook until golden and crispy – this will take about 2 minutes on each side.

4 Remove the bread from the grill and place on a serving dish.

5 Rub the cut edge of the garlic halves over the surface of the bruschetta, then top each slice with a spoonful of the tomato mixture. Serve immediately, garnishing each piece with a basil leaf and tomato rose.

TOMATO ROSES
To make this pretty garnish, using a small, sharp knife peel the skin of a firm-fleshed tomato in a continuous spiral, making it as long as possible. Roll it up, with the shiny side out, then gently adjust into a rose shape with your fingers.

"Only Italians could make something as ordinary as tomatoes on toast taste like sunshine." *Karen, Ipswich*

light meals

Smoked salmon 4

Who can resist this elegant dish? If you can find — and afford — traditional, hot-smoked wild salmon, you and your lucky guests will certainly notice the difference, but even farmed salmon is fabulous with scrambled eggs, hot buttered muffins and a squeeze of lemon.

SERVES 4

Preparation time: 10 minutes
Cooking time: 5 minutes

50 g/1¾ oz butter, plus extra
   for spreading
8 eggs, lightly beaten
4 tbsp double cream
225 g/8 oz skinless, boneless
   hot-smoked salmon, flaked
2 tbsp chopped fresh mixed
   herbs such as chives, basil
   and parsley
4 English muffins, split
salt and pepper

TO GARNISH
snipped fresh chives or parsley
lemon wedges
fresh flat-leaf parsley sprigs

VARIATION
If you have difficulty finding hot-smoked salmon, you could substitute conventional smoked salmon, chopped. Smoked rainbow trout would also make a good alternative, as it is usually hot-smoked and is widely available fresh or in vacuum packs.

1 Melt the butter in a large frying pan and when it begins to foam, add the eggs. Leave for a moment so they start to set, then slowly stir and move the set egg away from the base of the pan to allow the uncooked egg to take its place. Leave again for a moment and then repeat the process.

2 Before all the egg has set completely, stir in the double cream, flaked salmon and chopped herbs. Stir to incorporate. Make sure you do not overcook the eggs.

3 Meanwhile, toast the split muffins on both sides. Spread with more butter if liked. Place 2 muffin halves on each of 4 plates.

4 When the eggs are cooked, divide between the muffins. Scatter over a few snipped chives, season and serve while still warm, placing a lemon wedge garnished with a parsley sprig on each plate.

light meals

Cheese fondue

It's good to see the classic Swiss fondue returning to popularity — it's easy, inexpensive, delicious and delightful. As a traditional forfeit, you have to drink a glass of wine every time your dipper falls off the fork, so the evening should go with a swing.

SERVES 4

Preparation time: 10 minutes
Cooking time: 20 minutes

1 garlic clove, peeled and
   halved
425 ml/15 fl oz dry white wine
5 tbsp brandy
350 g/12 oz Gruyère cheese,
   grated
350 g/12 oz dolcelatte
   cheese, crumbled
1 tbsp cornflour
2 tbsp single cream
salt and pepper

DIPPERS
fresh crusty bread, cut into
   bite-sized pieces
bite-sized pieces of lightly
   cooked vegetables wrapped
   in cooked ham or strips of
   lightly cooked bacon

1 Rub the inside of a flameproof fondue pot with the garlic. Discard the garlic. Pour in the wine and 3 tablespoons of the brandy, then transfer to the hob and bring to a gentle simmer over a low heat. Add a small handful of the cheeses and stir constantly until melted. Continue to add the cheese gradually, stirring constantly after each addition, until all the cheese has been added. Continue to stir until thoroughly melted and bubbling gently.

2 Mix the cornflour with the remaining brandy in a small bowl. Stir the cornflour mixture into the fondue and continue to stir for 3–4 minutes until thickened and bubbling. Stir in the cream and season to taste with salt and pepper.

3 Using protective gloves, transfer the fondue pot to a lit tabletop burner. To serve, allow your guests to spear pieces of bread and ham-wrapped vegetables on to fondue forks and dip them into the fondue.

COOK'S TIP
It is important to add the cheese gradually and stir constantly until it has completely melted before adding any more. Otherwise, the mixture will 'split', that is, the fat will separate out. Keep the heat very low and, ideally, use an earthenware fondue pot rather than a metal one.

" This is the one for a girls' night in. It's lovely and messy, good for a giggle and everyone mucks in. "

Fiona, Dumfries

main courses

Lamb shanks

This bony cut from the end of the legs was once regarded as "cooks' perks" – cooks cleverly understanding how deliciously tender and flavoursome braising makes the meat. Now lamb shanks have become immensely fashionable in restaurants and on dinner party tables.

SERVES 6

Preparation time: 20 minutes
Marinating time: 4 hours
Cooking time: 3¾ hours

1 tsp coriander seeds

1 tsp cumin seeds

1 tsp ground cinnamon

1 fresh green chilli, deseeded
   and finely chopped

1 garlic bulb, separated into
   cloves

125 ml/4 fl oz groundnut or
   sunflower oil

grated rind of 1 lime

6 lamb shanks

2 onions, chopped

2 carrots, chopped

2 celery sticks, chopped

1 lime, chopped

about 700 ml/1¼ pints beef
   stock or water

1 tsp sun-dried tomato paste

2 fresh mint sprigs

2 fresh rosemary sprigs

salt and pepper

1 Dry-fry the coriander and cumin seeds until fragrant, then pound with the cinnamon, chilli and 2 garlic cloves in a pestle and mortar. Stir in half the oil and the lime rind. Rub the spice paste all over the lamb and marinate for 4 hours.

2 Preheat the oven to 200°C/ 400°F/Gas Mark 6. Heat the remaining oil in a flameproof casserole and cook the lamb, turning frequently, until evenly browned. Chop the remaining garlic and add to the casserole with the onions, carrots, celery and lime, then pour in enough stock or water to cover. Stir in the tomato paste, add the herbs and season with salt and pepper.

3 Cover and cook in the preheated oven for 30 minutes. Reduce the oven temperature to 160°C/325°F/Gas Mark 3 and cook for a further 3 hours, or until very tender.

4 Transfer the lamb to a dish and keep warm. Strain the cooking liquid into a saucepan and boil until reduced and thickened. Serve the lamb with the sauce poured over it.

COOK'S TIP
Dry-frying whole spices brings out their full flavour and aroma. Use a heavy-based frying pan over low to medium heat and shake frequently to prevent them from burning. As soon they begin to give off their fragrance and to pop, remove from the heat and tip into a mortar.

" Lamb shanks conjure up cosy nights in by the fire with loved ones. " *Jo, Surbiton*

main courses

Beef bourguignon 2

Lean beef slow-cooked with mushrooms, bacon and baby onions in red wine is a classic of French cuisine and a great dinner-party dish as it is so easy to make. Bear in mind that a poorly flavoured wine will not produce a fine-flavoured dish — cook with the same wine that you intend to serve.

SERVES 6

Preparation time: 20 minutes
Cooking time: 3¼ hours

2 tbsp olive oil

175 g/6 oz piece unsmoked
   bacon, sliced into thin strips

1.3 kg/3 lb braising steak, cut
   into 5 cm/2 inch pieces

2 carrots, sliced

2 onions, chopped

2 garlic cloves, very finely
   chopped

3 tbsp plain flour

700 ml/1¼ pints red wine

350–450 ml/12–16 fl oz beef
   stock

bouquet garni sachet
   (shop-bought)

1 tsp salt

¼ tsp pepper

3 tbsp butter

350 g/12 oz pickling onions

350 g/12 oz button mushrooms

2 tbsp chopped fresh parsley,
   to garnish

1 Heat the oil in a flameproof casserole and lightly brown the bacon for 2–3 minutes. Remove with a slotted spoon. Brown the beef in batches, drain and keep with the bacon. Soften the carrots and chopped onions in the same casserole for 5 minutes. Add the garlic and fry until just coloured. Return the meat and bacon to the casserole. Sprinkle on the flour and cook for 1 minute, stirring. Add the wine and enough stock to cover, the bouquet garni, salt and pepper. Bring to the boil, cover and simmer for 3 hours.

2 Melt half the butter in a frying pan, add the pickling onions, cover and cook until soft. Remove with a slotted spoon and keep warm. Fry the mushrooms in the remaining butter. Remove and keep warm.

3 Take the meat mixture and juices out of the casserole, sieving the juices into a pan. Wipe the casserole and tip in the meat, bacon, mushrooms and onions. Remove the surface fat from the cooking liquid, simmer for 1–2 minutes to reduce, then pour it over the meat and vegetables. Serve sprinkled with parsley.

" C'est magnifique et formidable!
You've got to hand it to the French —
they really know how to cook and how
to eat. **"** *Mark, Southampton*

> " The first meal my boyfriend made for a romantic Valentine's dinner – he's now my husband! "
>
> *Sharon, Weymouth*

main courses

Chicken kiev

Nothing to do with Russia, this crispy coated, succulent dish actually originated in France. There is, however, an art to cutting into it without causing hot garlic butter to spurt all over you — to be on the safe side, provide guests with very sharp knives and oversize napkins.

SERVES 4

Preparation time: 20 minutes
Chilling time: 30 minutes
Cooking time: 5–10 minutes

4 tbsp butter, softened

1 garlic clove, finely chopped

1 tbsp finely chopped fresh parsley

1 tbsp finely chopped fresh oregano

4 skinless, boneless chicken breasts

85 g/3 oz fresh white or wholemeal breadcrumbs

3 tbsp freshly grated Parmesan cheese

1 egg, beaten

250 ml/9 fl oz vegetable oil, for deep-frying

salt and pepper

TO GARNISH

slices of lemon

flat-leaf parsley sprigs

TO SERVE

freshly cooked new potatoes

selection of cooked vegetables

1 Place the butter and garlic in a bowl and mix together well. Stir in the chopped herbs and season well with salt and pepper. Pound the chicken breasts to flatten them to a even thickness, then place a tablespoon of herb butter in the centre of each one. Fold in the sides to enclose the butter, then secure with cocktail sticks.

2 Combine the breadcrumbs and grated Parmesan on a plate. Dip the chicken parcels into the beaten egg, then coat in the breadcrumb mixture. Transfer to a plate, cover and chill for 30 minutes. Remove from the refrigerator and coat in the egg and then the breadcrumb mixture for a second time.

3 Pour the oil into a deep-fat fryer to a depth that will cover the chicken parcels. Heat until it reaches 180–190°C/350–375°F, or until a cube of bread browns in 30 seconds. Transfer the chicken to the hot oil and deep-fry for 5 minutes, or until cooked through. Lift out the chicken and drain on kitchen paper.

4 Divide the chicken between 4 serving plates, garnish with lemon slices and parsley sprigs and serve with new potatoes and a selection of vegetables.

STEAMED VEGETABLES

For maximum flavour, colour and texture, steaming is one of the best ways of cooking vegetables. Mix together 55 g/2 oz butter, 1 tbsp chopped fresh parsley, 1 tbsp chopped fresh mint and season with salt and pepper. Reserve. Place a mixture of seasonal and colourful vegetables, such as broccoli florets, baby carrots, French beans and courgettes, in a steamer, season with salt and pepper, then cover and steam over a saucepan of boiling water for 5–7 minutes. Transfer to a warmed serving dish and dot with the herb butter. Potatoes can also be steamed and served in the same way; they take about 25 minutes. Don't peel them before cooking, but if you don't want to serve them with their skins on, peel them carefully afterwards.

main courses

Spaghetti alla carbonara

This is a wonderful dish for entertaining family and friends as it really is so easy and can be made in a matter of minutes. Make sure you add the eggs when the spaghetti is still hot as they must cook instantly to create a creamy texture.

SERVES 4

Preparation time: 10 minutes
Cooking time: 15 minutes

2 tbsp olive oil

1 tbsp butter

175 g/6 oz smoked streaky
  bacon, sliced into thin strips

3 eggs, lightly beaten

35 g/1¼ oz freshly grated
  Parmesan cheese

20 g/¾ oz pecorino cheese,
  grated

1 tbsp chopped fresh
  flat-leaf parsley

4 tbsp single cream

450 g/1 lb dried spaghetti

salt and pepper

1 Heat the oil and butter in a frying pan over a medium–high heat. Add the bacon and fry for 4–5 minutes until browned. Remove from the heat.

2 Combine the eggs, cheeses, parsley and cream in a bowl, mixing well. Season with pepper.

3 Cook the spaghetti in plenty of lightly salted boiling water until al dente. Drain and return the spaghetti quickly to the saucepan.

4 Add the egg mixture immediately to the spaghetti, tossing rapidly so that the egg cooks in the heat of the pasta. Transfer to a warmed serving dish.

5 Briefly reheat the bacon over a high heat. Add to the spaghetti, toss again and serve immediately.

" It's cheap, quick, easy and best of all, you know everyone will love it. **"**

Tony, Birmingham

main courses

Duck with orange

Regarded by many as the height of sophistication forty years ago, this is still a gorgeous combination as the sharpness and acidity of the citrus fruit cuts through and complements the richness of the meat. It always looks impressive and appetizing – perfect for dinner parties.

SERVES 4

Preparation time: 25 minutes
Cooking time: 30 minutes

4 boneless duck breasts

**freshly cooked julienned carrots
  and courgettes, to serve**

SAUCE

4 tbsp clear honey

2 tbsp orange juice

2 tsp soy sauce

1 Preheat the oven to 200°C/400°F/Gas Mark 6.

2 Score the skin of the duck breasts diagonally at 2.5 cm/ 1 inch intervals.

3 Heat a heavy griddle until it is smoking. Place the duck on the griddle, skin-side down, and cook for 5 minutes, or until starting to brown, over a high heat. Turn the duck over, reduce the heat and cook over a medium heat for a further 5 minutes.

4 Transfer the duck to a roasting tin, skin-side up, and place the tin in the preheated oven to cook for about 15 minutes.

5 While the duck is cooking, combine the honey, orange juice and soy sauce to make the sauce that will glaze the duck.

6 Remove the duck from the oven, pour over the sauce and return to the oven for a further 5 minutes.

7 Serve the duck breasts whole or thinly sliced, cut at an angle, with julienne of freshly cooked carrots and courgettes.

COOK'S TIP

Duck is a notoriously fatty meat, but modern breeding and farming methods produce much leaner birds than in the past. Barbary ducks, in particular, are much less fatty than more commonly available breeds and have a very distinctive flavour. However, they need careful cooking as the meat can dry out. Gressingham is another very popular breed for recipes that use only the breasts. The most widely available breed is the Aylesbury duck, although it is no longer farmed in the UK.

"First choice for a romantic, candlelit evening with the one you love."

Liz, Winchester

main courses

Spaghetti & meatballs

6

An Italian favourite that's ideal for hassle-free entertaining, especially if you have a mixed age group or lots of people to feed. It looks, smells and tastes terrific, kids love it and it's kind to the family budget. Plus, most of the preparation can be done in advance and the final cooking doesn't take very long. Perfetto!

SERVES 2

Preparation time: 15 minutes
Soaking time: 5 minutes
Cooking time: 55 minutes

2 thick slices crustless white bread

2 tbsp olive oil

1 red onion, chopped

2 garlic cloves, finely chopped

400 g/14 oz canned chopped tomatoes

8 basil leaves

2 tbsp tomato purée

1 tsp sugar

450 g/1 lb minced beef

2 eggs

1 tbsp chopped fresh parsley

1 tbsp chopped fresh basil

350 g/12 oz dried spaghetti

salt and pepper

freshly grated Parmesan cheese, to serve

1 Place the bread in a shallow dish and add just enough water to cover. Soak for 5 minutes, then drain and squeeze the bread to remove all the liquid.

2 Heat the oil in a saucepan, add the onion and half the garlic and cook over a medium heat, stirring occasionally, for 5 minutes. Add the tomatoes, with their juice, basil leaves, tomato purée and sugar and season with salt and pepper. Bring to the boil, reduce the heat and simmer, stirring occasionally, for 20 minutes until thickened and pulpy.

3 Mix the bread, beef, eggs, remaining herbs and garlic and ½ tsp of salt by hand in a large mixing bowl. Roll small pieces of the meat mixture into balls. Drop the meatballs into the tomato sauce, cover the saucepan and cook over a medium heat for 30 minutes.

4 Meanwhile, cook the spaghetti in a saucepan of lightly salted boiling water for 10 minutes, or until al dente. Drain well.

5 Transfer the spaghetti to a large shallow serving bowl. Arrange the meatballs and sauce on top. Sprinkle 2 tablespoons of freshly grated Parmesan cheese over the top and serve with more cheese in a bowl on the side.

COOK'S TIP

Al dente literally means 'to the tooth' and describes the texture of cooked pasta. The easiest way to test if the spaghetti is cooked to perfection is to remove a small piece from the saucepan and bite it between your front teeth. It should be tender but still firm to the bite. Pasta should never simmer, but boil quite vigorously. Bring a large saucepan of lightly salted water to the boil. Add the spaghetti, curling it into the water as it softens. Return to the boil and begin timing the cooking from this point. Start testing whether it is al dente about 2 minutes before the specified cooking time. Do not leave pasta standing around before serving or it will become tough and unpleasant. If, for some reason, the sauce is not ready, toss the spaghetti with a little olive oil or butter and keep warm.

main courses

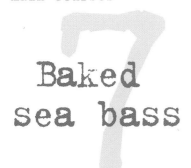

Baked sea bass

This magnificent steely grey fish has been every chef's choice for the past couple of decades and, now that it is widely available in supermarkets, it has become a decided favourite for dinner party hosts everywhere. Hardly surprising – it looks and tastes superb.

SERVES 4

Preparation time: 20 minutes
Cooking time: 30–50 minutes

1.3 kg/3 lb fresh sea bass or
    2 x 750 g/1 lb 10 oz sea bass,
    gutted
2–4 fresh rosemary sprigs
½ lemon, thinly sliced
2 tbsp olive oil

GARLIC SAUCE

2 tsp coarse sea salt
2 tsp capers
2 garlic cloves, crushed
4 tbsp water
2 bay leaves
1 tsp lemon juice or
    wine vinegar
2 tbsp olive oil
pepper

TO GARNISH

bay leaves
lemon wedges

1 Preheat the oven to 190°C/375°F/Gas Mark 5.

2 Scrape off the scales from the fish and cut off the sharp fins. Make diagonal cuts along both sides. Wash and dry thoroughly. Place a rosemary sprig in the cavity of each of the smaller fish with half the lemon slices; or 2 sprigs and all the lemon in the large fish.

3 Place the fish in a foil-lined dish or roasting tin brushed with oil, and brush the fish with the rest of the oil. Cook in the preheated oven for 30 minutes for the small fish or 45–50 minutes if using the large fish, until the thickest part of the fish is opaque.

4 To make the sauce, crush the salt and capers with the garlic in a pestle and mortar, then work in the water. Alternatively, work in a food processor or blender until smooth.

5 Bruise the bay leaves and remaining rosemary sprigs and place in a bowl. Add the garlic mixture, lemon juice and oil and pound together until the flavours are released. Season to taste with pepper.

6 Place the fish on a serving dish and, if preferred, remove the skin. Spoon some of the sauce over the fish and serve the rest separately. Garnish with bay leaves and lemon wedges.

COOK'S TIP
Use a fish scaler or small serrated knife to scale the sea bass. Work from the tail towards the head and rinse frequently under cold running water. Use strong kitchen scissors to cut off the fins, taking particular care with the spiny first dorsal fin.

main courses

Moules à la marinière

This always comes high on the list for lovers of seafood. Surrounded by a richly flavoured sauce, the orange flesh of the mussels resting in their dark half-shells looks every bit as good as it tastes. Lots of finger bowls are required for this truly messy delight.

SERVES 4

Preparation time: 15 minutes
Cooking time: 5 minutes

2 kg/4 lb 8 oz live mussels

300 ml/10 fl oz dry white wine

6 shallots, chopped

bouquet garni sachet

 (shop-bought)

pepper

French bread, to serve

1 Scrub the mussels under cold water and pull of their 'beards' with your fingers or using a small, sharp knife. Discard any with broken or damaged shells or any that do not shut immediately when sharply tapped with the back of a knife.

2 Pour the wine into a large saucepan or flameproof casserole, add the shallots and bouquet garni and season to taste with pepper. Bring to the boil over a medium heat, then add the mussels, cover tightly and cook, shaking the saucepan occasionally, for about 5 minutes, or until all the mussels have opened.

3 Remove and discard the bouquet garni sachet and any mussels that remain shut. Using a slotted spoon, divide the mussels between 4 soup plates or bowls. Tilt the saucepan to allow any sand to settle, then spoon the cooking liquid over the mussels. Serve immediately with French bread.

VARIATION

For a richer sauce, cook the mussels as described here, but strain the cooking liquid through a very fine sieve or muslin into a clean saucepan. Bring to the boil and reduce by about half. Stir in 100 ml/3½ fl oz double cream. Return the mussels to the saucepan, heat through again very briefly and serve, garnished with chopped parsley.

COOK'S TIP
All shellfish should always be eaten on the day of purchase, as they deteriorate very rapidly. It is important to discard any mussels that do not close when you are preparing them and any that have not opened during cooking. These were dead before you started and could cause food poisoning.

" Reminds me of fond memories I have of long summer holidays in the south of France with my family. My sister and I would order it and a big piece of baguette in a little local restaurant on the harbour. "

Alexandra, Stockport

"I love making pasta — it's just as therapeutic as yoga. I love serving it to my friends too." *Gina, Bath*

main courses

Tortellini

Virtually everyone loves pasta, especially home-made stuffed pasta. Who could resist these bite-sized morsels that are said to be designed to mimic the shape of Venus's navel? How did they know what it looked like? Nevertheless, this is sensuous food for a special occasion.

SERVES 4

Preparation time: 45 minutes
Resting time: 30 minutes
Cooking time: 25–30 minutes

115 g/4 oz boneless chicken
  breast, skinned

55 g/2 oz Parma ham

40 g/1½ oz cooked spinach,
  well drained

1 tbsp finely chopped onion

2 tbsp freshly grated
  Parmesan cheese

pinch of ground allspice

1 egg, beaten

450 g/1 lb basic pasta dough

salt and pepper

2 tbsp chopped fresh parsley,
  to garnish

SAUCE

300 ml/10 fl oz single cream

2 garlic cloves, crushed

115 g/4 oz button mushrooms,
  thinly sliced

4 tbsp freshly grated Parmesan
  cheese

1 Bring a saucepan of lightly salted water to the boil. Add the chicken and poach for 10 minutes. Cool slightly, then place in a food processor, with the Parma ham, spinach and onion and process until finely chopped. Stir in the Parmesan cheese, allspice and egg and season to taste with salt and pepper.

2 Thinly roll out the pasta dough and cut into 4–5 cm/1½–2 inch rounds.

3 Place ½ tsp of the filling in the centre of each round. Fold the pieces in half and press the edges to seal. Then wrap each piece around your index finger, cross over the ends and curl the rest of the dough backwards to make a navel shape. Re-roll the trimmings and repeat until all the dough is used up.

4 Bring a saucepan of lightly salted water to the boil. Add the tortellini, in batches, return to the boil and cook for 5 minutes. Drain and transfer to a serving dish.

5 To make the sauce, bring the cream and garlic to the boil in a small saucepan, then simmer for 3 minutes. Add the mushrooms and half the Parmesan cheese, season to taste with salt and pepper and simmer for 2–3 minutes. Pour the sauce over the tortellini. Sprinkle over the remaining Parmesan cheese, garnish with parsley and serve immediately.

PASTA DOUGH

To make the dough by hand, sift 200 g/7 oz plain flour and a pinch of salt on to a clean work surface. Make a well in the centre and add 2 lightly beaten eggs and 1 tbsp olive oil. Using your fingers, gradually incorporate the flour into the liquid. Knead the dough thoroughly until smooth, then wrap in clingfilm and leave to rest in the refrigerator for 30 minutes. Alternatively, sift the flour and salt into a food processor. Add the eggs and oil and process until the mixture just comes together. Turn out and knead until smooth, then wrap and chill for 30 minutes.

main courses

Coq au vin

Invented by French peasants to make tough old birds palatable, this superb stew has become a mainstay of dinner party menus. Tenderizing chicken is no longer the problem, but giving it a special flavour is a little more difficult - this recipe is brilliant.

SERVES 4

Preparation time: 10 minutes
Cooking time: 1¼ hours

2 tbsp butter

8 baby onions

125 g/4½ oz streaky bacon,
   roughly chopped

4 chicken joints

1 garlic clove, finely chopped

12 button mushrooms

300 ml/10 fl oz red wine

bouquet garni sachet
   (shop-bought)

1 tbsp chopped fresh tarragon

2 tsp cornflour

1–2 tbsp cold water

salt and pepper

fresh flat-leaf parsley
   sprigs, to garnish

sautéed sliced potatoes,
   to serve

1 Melt half of the butter in a large frying pan over a medium heat. Add the onions and bacon and cook, stirring, for 3 minutes. Lift out the bacon and onions and reserve.

2 Melt the remaining butter in the frying pan and add the chicken joints. Cook for 3 minutes, then turn over and cook on the other side for 2 minutes. Drain off some of the chicken fat before returning the bacon and onions to the pan. Then add the garlic, mushrooms, red wine, bouquet garni and tarragon. Season to taste with salt and pepper. Cook for about 1 hour, or until the chicken is cooked through.

3 Remove the frying pan from the heat, lift out the chicken, onions, bacon and mushrooms, transfer them to a serving platter and keep warm. Discard the bouquet garni.

4 Mix the cornflour with enough of the water to make a paste, then stir into the juices in the frying pan. Bring to the boil, reduce the heat and cook, stirring, for 1 minute. Pour the sauce over the chicken, garnish with parsley sprigs and serve with sautéed sliced potatoes.

ACCOMPANIMENTS

Coq au vin is almost a meal in itself and needs little in the way of extras. Fresh bread is essential for mopping up the sauce and it does go well with salad, either served at the same time or, French-style, afterwards. For a classic lettuce and herb salad, tear a mixture of salad leaves, such as oakleaf, frisée, radicchio and rocket, into bite-sized pieces and place in a bowl. Peel half a cucumber, cut it in half lengthways and scoop out the seeds with a teaspoon. Slice thinly and add to the leaves. Add 4 tbsp chopped mixed herbs, such as parsley, thyme and chives and toss well. Using a fork, whisk together 1 tbsp white wine vinegar and 1 tsp Dijon mustard in a small bowl. Gradually whisk in 4 tbsp extra virgin olive oil and season to taste with salt and pepper. Just before serving, pour the dressing over the salad and toss lightly.

" I cooked Coq au Vin for my parents
to impress them when I was about 14 —
only to get told off for using the last
bottle of the expensive wine my Dad had
bought on holiday in France! "

Daniel, Neath

" Profiteroles always remind me of the first time my boyfriend took me out for a surprise romantic dinner... "   *Emily, Canvey Island*

desserts

Profiteroles

1

A pyramid of little chocolate-covered puffs of choux pastry makes a striking centrepiece on the dinner table and looks almost too pretty to eat. However, you can bet that even your skinniest and most health-conscious friends will still throw caution to the wind.

SERVES 4

Preparation time: 25 minutes
Cooking time: 35 minutes
Cooling time: 30 minutes

CHOUX PASTRY

5 tbsp butter, plus extra for
  greasing

200 ml/7 fl oz cold water

100 g/3½ oz plain flour

3 eggs, beaten

CREAM FILLING

300 ml/10 fl oz double cream

3 tbsp caster sugar

1 tsp vanilla essence

CHOCOLATE & BRANDY SAUCE

125 g/4½ oz plain dark
  chocolate, broken into pieces

2½ tbsp butter

6 tbsp water

2 tbsp brandy

1 Preheat the oven to 200°C/400°F/Gas Mark 6.

2 Grease a large baking sheet with butter. To make the pastry, place the water and butter in a saucepan and bring to the boil. Meanwhile, sift the flour into a bowl. Remove the saucepan from the heat and beat in the flour until smooth. Cool for 5 minutes. Beat in enough of the eggs to give the mixture a soft, dropping consistency. Transfer to a piping bag fitted with a 1-cm/½-inch plain nozzle. Pipe small balls onto the baking sheet. Bake for 25 minutes.

Remove from the oven. Pierce each ball with a skewer in order to let steam escape.

3 To make the filling, whip together the cream, sugar and vanilla essence. Cut the pastry balls almost in half, then fill with cream.

4 To make the sauce, gently melt the chocolate and butter with the water in a small saucepan, stirring, until smooth. Stir in the brandy. Pile the profiteroles into individual serving dishes or into a pyramid on a raised cake stand. Pour over the sauce and serve.

desserts

Crème brûlée tarts

Caramelized sugar makes a contrasting and decorative topping on the creamy, melt-in-the-mouth filling in these tarts. It's funny that we all think crème brûlée is French because it was actually invented in the English university town of Cambridge.

SERVES 6

Preparation time: 25 minutes
Chilling time: 11 hours
Cooking time: 30 minutes
Cooling time: 30 minutes

PASTRY

150 g/5½ oz plain flour, plus
    extra for dusting
25 g/1 oz caster sugar
125 g/4½ oz butter, cut into
    small pieces
1 tbsp water
demerara sugar, for sprinkling

FILLING

4 egg yolks
50 g/1¾ oz caster sugar
400 ml/14 fl oz double cream
1 tsp vanilla essence

1 To make the pastry, place the flour and sugar in a bowl and rub in the butter with your fingers. Add the water and work the mixture together until a soft pastry has formed. Wrap in clingfilm and leave to chill for 30 minutes.

2 Roll out the dough on a lightly floured work surface and use to line 6 x 10-cm/4-inch tart tins. Prick the base of the pastry with a fork and leave to chill for 20 minutes.

3 Preheat the oven to 190°C/375°F/Gas Mark 5. Line the pastry cases with foil and baking beans and bake in the oven for 15 minutes. Remove the foil and beans and cook for a further 10 minutes until crisp and golden. Leave to cool.

4 Meanwhile, make the filling. In a bowl, beat the egg yolks and caster sugar until thick and pale. Heat the cream and vanilla essence in a saucepan until just below boiling point, then pour it onto the egg mixture, whisking constantly.

5 Return the mixture to a clean saucepan and bring to just below boiling point, stirring, until thick. Do not boil or it will curdle.

6 Leave the mixture to cool slightly, then pour it into the tart tins. Leave to cool and then leave to chill overnight.

7 Preheat the grill to medium. Sprinkle the tarts with the sugar. Place under the hot grill for a few minutes until browned on top. Cool, then chill for 2 hours before serving.

COOK'S TIP

The secret of crisp, light pastry is to handle it as little as possible. When you're rubbing in the butter, use only the tips of your fingers. The palms of your hands will warm up and partially melt the butter. If it's a hot day – or the kitchen is well heated – rinse your hands under cold running water, then dry before you start. Place the water for mixing the dough in the refrigerator to chill.

> " I rate individual desserts
> because you don't have to
> concentrate on cutting equal
> slices when you've had a couple
> of glasses of wine. "

Anne-Marie, Dover

desserts

Pavlova

Named in tribute to the incomparable Russian ballerina after she visited Australia in 1929, this is another dessert that is almost too lovely to divide into portions. A light-as-air, crisp meringue base is topped with a beautifully luscious mixture of cream and fruit.

SERVES 4

Preparation time: 30 minutes
Cooking time: 3 hours
Cooling time: 30 minutes

6 egg whites

pinch of cream of tartar

pinch of salt

275 g/9¾ oz caster sugar

600 ml/1 pint double cream

1 tsp vanilla essence

2 kiwi fruits, peeled and sliced

250 g/9 oz strawberries, hulled
 and sliced

3 ripe peaches, sliced

1 ripe mango, peeled and sliced

2 tbsp orange liqueur, such
 as Cointreau

fresh mint leaves, to decorate

1 Preheat the oven to 110°C/225°F/Gas Mark ¼. Line 3 baking sheets with baking paper, then draw a 22-cm/8½-inch circle in the centre of each one. Beat the egg whites into stiff peaks. Mix in the cream of tartar and salt. Gradually add 200 g/7 oz of the sugar. Beat for 2 minutes until glossy. Fill a piping bag with the meringue mixture and pipe enough to fill each circle, doming them slightly in the centre. Bake for 3 hours. Remove from the oven. Leave to cool.

2 Whip together the cream and vanilla essence with the remaining sugar. Put the fruit into a separate bowl and stir in the liqueur. Put one meringue circle onto a plate, then spread over one-third of the sugared cream. Spread over one-third of the fruit, then top with a meringue circle. Spread over another third of cream, then another third of fruit. Top with the last meringue circle. Spread over the remaining cream, followed by the rest of the fruit. Decorate with mint leaves and serve.

COOK'S TIP
It is essential that the bowl used for mixing egg whites is completely free of grease. It is difficult to ensure this with plastic, but glass, ceramic or stainless steel work well. The best material is copper which reacts with egg whites to produce a firm foam. However, do not leave whisked whites standing in a copper bowl as they will turn an unappealing shade of grey. Aluminium is not a suitable material.

desserts

Black Forest 4 gâteau

Fresh cherries, sweetened cream, a lacing of liqueur and a profusion of chocolate, this elegant layered cake – Schwarzwälder Kirschtorte to give it its Bavarian name – has quite rightly featured on British dinner-party menus for at least fifty years

SERVES 8

Preparation time: 25 minutes
Cooking time: 55 minutes
Cooling time: 45 minutes

3 tbsp unsalted butter, melted,
  plus extra for greasing
900 g/2 lb fresh cherries, stoned
  and halved
250 g/9 oz caster sugar
100 ml/3½ fl oz cherry brandy
100 g/3½ oz plain flour
50 g/1¾ oz cocoa powder
½ tsp baking powder
4 eggs
1 litre/1¾ pints double cream

TO DECORATE
grated plain dark chocolate
whole fresh cherries

1 Preheat the oven to 180°C/350°F/Gas Mark 4. Grease and line a 23-cm/9-inch springform cake tin. Place the cherries in a saucepan, add 3 tablespoons of the sugar and the cherry brandy. Simmer for 5 minutes. Drain, reserving the syrup. In another bowl, sift together the flour, cocoa and baking powder.

2 Place the eggs in a heatproof bowl and beat in 160 g/5¾ oz of the sugar. Place the bowl over a saucepan of simmering water and beat for 6 minutes, or until thickened. Remove from the heat, then gradually fold in the flour mixture and melted butter. Spoon into the cake tin and bake for 40 minutes. Remove from the oven and leave to cool.

3 Turn out the cake and cut in half horizontally. Mix the cream and the remaining sugar together and whip lightly. Spread the reserved syrup over the cut sides of the cake, then top with a layer of cream on each side. Arrange the cherries over one half of the cake, then place the other half on top of it. Cover the whole cake with cream, press grated chocolate all over the surface and decorate with whole fresh cherries.

COOK'S TIP
Any cherry-flavoured liqueur can be used in this cake or you could use kirsch, which is a cherry eau-de-vie. As it's such a luxurious recipe, it's worth buying the best quality chocolate for the decoration and grating it yourself rather than using ready grated.

desserts

Chocolate mousses

A dessert to die for, these delightful individual mousses display all the simple chic of classic French cuisine. Use the best-quality chocolate you can find to ensure a rich and rewarding flavour and rummage in the cupboard for your prettiest dishes for the most elegant presentation.

SERVES 4

Preparation time: 20 minutes
Cooking time: 5 minutes
Chilling time: 4 hours

300 g/10½ oz plain dark
   chocolate

1½ tbsp unsalted butter

1 tbsp brandy

4 eggs, separated

cocoa powder, for dusting

1 Break the chocolate into small pieces and place in a heatproof bowl set over a pan of simmering water. Add the butter and melt with the chocolate, stirring, until smooth. Remove from the heat, stir in the brandy and leave to cool slightly. Add the egg yolks and beat until smooth.

2 In a separate bowl, whisk the egg whites until stiff peaks have formed, then fold them into the chocolate mixture. Put 4 stainless steel cooking rings on 4 small serving plates, then spoon the mixture into the rings and level the surfaces. Transfer to the refrigerator and chill for at least 4 hours until set.

3 Take the mousses out of the refrigerator and remove the cooking rings. Dust with cocoa powder and serve.

COOK'S TIP
For an even prettier decoration, you can use icing sugar and cocoa powder. Gently cover part of each mousse with a piece of cardboard and sift icing sugar over the exposed surface. Then cover the icing sugar and sift cocoa powder over the undecorated part.

" Delicious? Magical? Fabulous? Bodacious? There's no word in the English language to describe chocolate mousse. "

Pat, Bournemouth

"My mum always made lots of traditional classics, and Tapioca pudding always brings back warm memories of family dinners and the special times that we shared round the dinner table."

Amy, Dundee

EVERYDAY ESSENTIALS

Jacket potatoes, presented here with a creamy walnut filling, is a run-away winner for light meals. 'Spag bol' took the gold medal for a main course, while carrot cake came top of the desserts.

light meals

Jacket potatoes

There is an almost endless variety of fillings for jacket potatoes. This recipe uses potatoes filled with a delicious combination of cream, cheese, mushrooms and walnuts. It's an almost effortless snack at any time of day, or it can be served with a simple salad for a lovely light lunch.

SERVES 4

Preparation time: 15 minutes
Cooking time: 1½ hours

4 large baking potatoes

85 g/3 oz butter

1 large garlic clove, crushed

150 g/5½ oz mushrooms, sliced

1 tbsp snipped fresh chives

2 tbsp chopped fresh parsley

175 ml/6 fl oz double cream

4 tbsp Cheddar cheese, grated

salt and pepper

4 tbsp chopped lightly toasted
  walnuts, to garnish

fresh mixed salad, to serve

1 Preheat the oven to 190°C/375°F/Gas Mark 5. Scrub the potatoes and pierce the skins several times with a fork. Place on a baking tray and cook in the preheated oven for 1¼ hours, or until cooked through.

2 About 5 minutes before the end of the cooking time, melt 1½ tablespoons of the butter in a frying pan over a low heat. Add the garlic and mushrooms and cook, stirring, for 4 minutes, or until the mushrooms are tender. Remove the frying pan from the heat and reserve until required.

3 Remove the potatoes from the oven and cut them in half lengthways. Carefully scoop out the potato flesh into a bowl, leaving the skins intact. Add the remaining butter to the potato flesh, then stir in the herbs. Season to taste with salt and pepper. Spoon the mixture into the potato skins, then add a layer of mushrooms. Top with the cream, then the cheese. Return the potatoes to the oven and bake for a further 10 minutes at the same temperature.

4 Remove from the oven, scatter over the walnuts and serve with a mixed salad.

" This is fireside food when the rain's pouring down and your favourite movie's on TV. "

Rachel, Belfast

light meals

Salad

With so many delicious salads voted for, selecting one was very difficult, but in the end we've plumped for Salad Niçoise. It incorporates all the delicious sunshine ingredients of the famously healthy and delicious Mediterranean diet — tomatoes, peppers, olives, anchovies and tuna.

SERVES 4

Preparation time: 20 minutes
Cooking time: 10 minutes
Cooling time: 20 minutes

4 eggs

200 g/7 oz French beans

1 green pepper, deseeded and
  sliced

4 tomatoes, cut into wedges

1 red onion, halved and sliced

1 tbsp chopped fresh parsley

1 tbsp chopped fresh coriander

50 g/1¾ oz black olives, stoned

400 g/14 oz canned tuna in
  brine

50 g/1¾ oz anchovy fillets
  in oil

DRESSING

5 tbsp extra virgin olive oil

3 tbsp red wine vinegar

½ tsp clear honey

1 garlic clove, finely chopped

salt and pepper

TO GARNISH

capers

flat-leaf parsley sprigs

1 Bring 2 saucepans of water to the boil. Add the eggs to one pan, return to the boil, reduce the heat and cook for 10 minutes. While the eggs are cooking, trim the French beans and put them in the other pan. Bring to the boil and blanch for 3 minutes, then drain and plunge into cold water. Drain again and leave to cool. When the eggs are cooked, drain and plunge them into cold water. Drain again and leave to cool.

2 To make the dressing, combine all the ingredients in a small bowl. Season and stir together well.

3 Divide the pepper, tomatoes, onion, parsley and coriander between 4 serving dishes. Halve the olives and the French beans, shell and quarter the eggs, and add them all to the salads. Drain the tuna and anchovies and add to the salads. Drizzle over the dressing and garnish with capers and parsley sprigs. Cover with clingfilm and chill in the refrigerator until required.

VARIATION

This salad is also great made with a fresh tuna fillet weighing about 350–450 g/12 oz–1 lb. Brush both sides with olive oil and season well with salt and pepper. Heat a griddle pan until it is very hot, then add the tuna and cook on both sides. If you like your fish raw to rare in the centre, cook for 2 minutes on each side, increasing the time to about 5 minutes each side if you prefer it well done. Season with salt and pepper again before slicing and adding to the salad.

light meals

Soup

Tomato soup is one of the nation's all-time favourites, and here is the real thing. Home-made soup doesn't have to be a time-consuming and laborious process for the results to be out of this world. Serve it on its own as a first course or with crusty bread for a filling Saturday lunch.

SERVES 4

Preparation time: 10 minutes
Cooking time: 30–35 minutes

1 tbsp olive oil

2 tbsp water

2 red peppers, deseeded and finely chopped

1 garlic clove, finely chopped

1 onion, finely chopped

400 g/14 oz canned chopped tomatoes

1.2 litres/2 pints vegetable stock

salt and pepper

fresh basil leaves, to garnish

1 Place the oil, water, peppers, garlic and onion in a saucepan, heat gently and cook for 5–10 minutes, or until the vegetables have softened. Cover the saucepan and simmer for a further 10 minutes.

2 Add the tomatoes, stock, salt and pepper and simmer, uncovered, for 15 minutes.

3 Serve the soup garnished with basil leaves.

COOK'S TIP

If you are using stock cubes or powder, take care with the seasoning as some brands are already extremely salty. Home-made stock is the ideal choice. It can be prepared quite quickly and stored in the freezer. Heat 2 tbsp sunflower oil in a large saucepan and add 115 g/4 oz finely chopped onions and 115 g/4 oz finely chopped leeks. Cook over a low heat, stirring occasionally, for 5 minutes until softened. Add 85 g/3 oz finely chopped carrots, 2 finely chopped celery sticks and 2 finely chopped tomatoes and cook, stirring occasionally, for a further 10 minutes. Add a bouquet garni sachet and pour in 2.5 litres/4½ pints water. Bring to the boil, then simmer for 20 minutes. Strain into a bowl and season with salt and pepper.

"A cosy warm glowing feeling you only get from home cooking on a cold winter's day: sitting by the open fire having hot soup and bread."

Mary, Carshalton

66 When it's my turn to cook, this is my favourite recipe — it makes me feel like a real chef. My wife loves it too. 99 *Rod, Ealing*

light meals

Omelette

When it comes to omelettes, there is nothing quite as delicious and filling as a Spanish omelette. Cut into wedges and served with a glass of chilled wine, this tasty potato and vegetable omelette makes a lovely summer lunch or light supper. You can experiment with other vegetables too.

SERVES 4

Preparation time: 10 minutes, plus pre-cooking the vegetables
Cooking time: 15 minutes
Resting time: 5 minutes

115 g/4 oz butter

1 small onion, chopped

115 g/4 oz cooked diced
  potatoes or pasta

55 g/2 oz cooked peas,
  sweetcorn or diced courgettes

115 g/4 oz cooked asparagus,
  cut into 2.5 cm/1 inch pieces,
  or chopped spinach

8 large eggs

4 tbsp milk

1 tbsp tomato purée

175 g/6 oz Manchego or mature
  Cheddar cheese, grated

salt and pepper

salad, to serve

1 Melt the butter in a large frying pan over a medium heat. Add the onion, stir well and cook for 3–4 minutes until softened.

2 Mix in the potatoes or pasta and remaining vegetables and cook for a further 2 minutes to heat through.

3 Beat the eggs in a mixing bowl with the milk, tomato purée, salt and pepper. Pour over the vegetables and reduce the heat to low. Cook for 5 minutes, occasionally lifting the edges and tilting the frying pan to let the liquid run underneath.

4 Preheat the grill until it has reached a high temperature. When the eggs are almost set, sprinkle over the cheese. Place the frying pan under the hot grill and cook for 2 minutes until the cheese has melted and is golden brown.

5 Remove the frying pan from the grill and leave the omelette to rest for 5 minutes. Transfer to a large serving dish and serve, cut in wedges, with salad.

COOK'S TIP
You can also cook the omelette in a preheated oven, 150°C/300°F/Gas Mark 2 for about 15 minutes. It should be quite crisp and golden on the outside but still slightly wobbly in the centre.

light meals

Noodles

Quick to cook, noodles have long been a popular base for a quick and easy dish. This marinated steak recipe is an Asian speciality that will add variety to weekday menus. You can use a different type of noodle if you prefer – just follow the instructions on the packet.

SERVES 4

Preparation time: 10 minutes
Marinating time: 1 hour
Cooking time: 8 minutes

MARINADE

1 tsp dry sherry

1 tbsp soy sauce

1 tbsp groundnut oil

1 tsp sesame oil

1 tsp cornflour

2 tsp clear honey

1 shallot, finely chopped

STIR-FRY

280 g/10 oz rump steak, cut
   into strips

300 ml/10 fl oz vegetable oil,
   to deep-fry the noodles

225 g/8 oz rice noodles

1 tbsp soy sauce

1 tbsp black bean sauce

1 tsp cornflour

125 ml/4 fl oz water

TO GARNISH

8 spring onions, thinly sliced

flat-leaf parsley sprigs

1 To make the marinade, mix the sherry, soy sauce, groundnut oil, sesame oil, cornflour, honey and shallot together in a large bowl. Add the steak and toss to coat. Cover with clingfilm and chill for 1 hour.

2 Heat the vegetable oil in a frying pan or wok over a high heat until very hot. Using a metal sieve, lower the noodles into the oil for 3 seconds until they are puffed up. Remove carefully, let the oil drain from the sieve and set the noodles aside to drain on kitchen paper.

3 Take 5 tablespoons of oil from the frying pan and heat in a second frying pan or wok. Remove the marinated steak from the refrigerator, add to the frying pan and stir-fry over a medium heat, for 3–4 minutes. Remove the steak from the frying pan and reserve.

4 Add the soy sauce, black bean sauce, cornflour and water to the oil in the second frying pan and cook gently until the mixture boils. Add the steak and cook for 1 minute. Remove from the heat. Snap the noodles into shorter lengths and place on a serving dish. Top with the steak, garnish with spring onions and parsley and serve immediately.

COOK'S TIP
Sesame oil is widely available from supermarkets. It is made from cold-pressed sesame seeds and has a very distinctive flavour and aroma. As it burns very easily, it is usually used for flavouring rather than for cooking. Toasted sesame oil is becoming increasingly popular and can be bought at Chinese supermarkets and some larger shops. It is a deeper golden colour than the fresh oil, but also burns easily.

“ The first proper dinner my baby daughter ate, and one of the meals the whole family enjoys. **”**

Catherine, Aylesbury

main courses

Spaghetti bolognese

This is the British version of an Italian classic — in Bologna they always use tagliatelle and the preparation of the ragú, meat sauce, is more time consuming. It is a perennial favourite with all ages, so it's no surprise that it is the number one choice in this category.

SERVES 4

Preparation time: 15 minutes
Cooking time: 1¼ hours

2 tbsp olive oil

1 tbsp butter

1 small onion, finely chopped

1 carrot, finely chopped

1 celery stick, finely chopped

50 g/1¾ oz mushrooms, diced

225 g/8 oz fresh beef mince

75 g/2¾ oz unsmoked bacon
  or ham, diced

2 chicken livers, chopped

2 tbsp tomato purée

125 ml/4 fl oz dry white wine

½ tsp freshly grated nutmeg

300 ml/10 fl oz chicken stock

125 ml/4 fl oz double cream

450 g/1 lb dried spaghetti

salt and pepper

2 tbsp chopped fresh parsley,
  to garnish

freshly grated Parmesan
  cheese, to serve

1 Heat the oil and butter in a large saucepan over a medium heat. Add the onion, carrot, celery and mushrooms to the pan, then fry until softened. Add the beef mince and bacon to the saucepan and fry until the mince is evenly browned.

2 Stir in the chicken livers and tomato purée and cook for 2–3 minutes. Pour in the wine and season with salt, pepper and nutmeg. Add the stock. Bring to the boil, then cover and simmer gently over a low heat for 1 hour. Stir in the cream and simmer, uncovered, until reduced.

3 Cook the spaghetti in plenty of lightly salted boiling water until al dente. Drain and transfer to a warmed serving dish.

4 Spoon the sauce over the top of the pasta. Garnish with the parsley and serve with freshly grated Parmesan cheese.

main courses

Lasagne verde

Alternate layers of spinach pasta and sauce smothered in a Parmesan-topped, creamy béchamel, then baked in the oven, make a filling and fabulous supper dish. You won't need to add anything else except, maybe, a glass of wine for the adults in the family.

SERVES 4

Preparation time: 25 minutes
Cooking time: 2¼–2½ hours

1 tbsp olive oil

225 g/8 oz lasagne verde (fresh
  or dried)

butter, for greasing

60 g/2¼ oz freshly grated
  Parmesan cheese

salt and pepper

green salad, tomato salad or
  black olives, to serve

RAGÙ

3 tbsp olive oil

45 g/1½ oz butter

2 large onions, chopped

4 celery sticks, thinly sliced

175 g/6 oz streaky bacon,
  chopped

2 garlic cloves, chopped

500 g/1 lb 2 oz fresh beef mince

2 tbsp tomato purée

1 tbsp plain flour

400 g/14 oz canned chopped
  tomatoes

150 ml/5 fl oz beef stock

150 ml/5 fl oz red wine

2 tsp dried oregano

½ tsp freshly grated nutmeg

BÉCHAMEL SAUCE

300 ml/10 fl oz milk

2 bay leaves

3 cloves

1 small onion

60 g/2¼ oz butter

40 g/1½ oz plain flour

300 ml/10 fl oz single cream

large pinch of freshly grated
  nutmeg

salt and pepper

1 To make the ragù, heat the oil and butter in a large frying pan over a medium heat. Add the onions, celery and bacon and fry for 5 minutes, stirring. Stir in the garlic and beef mince and cook, stirring until the meat has lost its redness. Reduce the heat and cook for 10 minutes, stirring. Increase the heat to medium, stir in the tomato purée and the flour and cook for 1–2 minutes. Stir in the tomatoes, stock and wine and bring to the boil, stirring. Season with salt and pepper and stir in the oregano and nutmeg. Simmer uncovered, stirring, for 55 minutes–1 hour, or until the mixture is reduced to a thick paste.

2 Have ready a large saucepan of lightly salted boiling water and add the olive oil. Drop the pasta sheets into the boiling water a few at a time, and return the water to the boil before adding further pasta sheets. If you are using fresh lasagne, cook the sheets for a total of 8 minutes. If you are using dried pasta, cook it according to the packet instructions.

3 Remove the pasta sheets from the saucepan with a slotted spoon. Spread them in a single layer on damp tea towels.

4 Meanwhile, make the béchamel sauce. Pour the milk into a small saucepan and add the bay leaves. Press the cloves into the onion, add

" This is the one meal that I know everyone in the family will eat – even the dog gets to lick the plates. "

Mary, Wellingborough

to the saucepan and bring the milk to the boil. Remove from the heat and leave to cool. Strain the milk into a jug and rinse the saucepan. Melt the butter in the saucepan and stir in the flour. Stir for 1 minute, then gradually pour in the milk, stirring. Cook the sauce for 3 minutes, then pour in the cream and bring to the boil. Remove from the heat and season to taste with nutmeg, salt and pepper.

5 Preheat the oven to 190°C/375°F/Gas Mark 5. Grease a rectangular ovenproof dish, about 25–28 cm/10–11 inches long. To assemble the dish, spoon a little of the meat sauce into the prepared dish, cover with a layer of lasagne, then spoon over a little béchamel sauce and sprinkle with some of the cheese. Continue making layers in this way, covering

the final layer of lasagne with the remaining béchamel sauce.

6 Sprinkle on the remaining cheese and bake in the preheated oven for 40 minutes, or until the sauce is golden brown and bubbling. Serve with a green salad, a tomato salad or a bowl of black olives.

main courses

Stir-fry

This spicy stir-fry recipe hails from India; with their long tradition of vegetarianism, Indian cooks really know how to get the best out of vegetables. Speedy stir-frying and a subtle blend of spices make for everyday ease but exceptional flavour. Serve with boiled rice or naan bread.

SERVES 4

Preparation time: 10 minutes
Cooking time: 15 minutes

3 tbsp vegetable oil

½ tsp ground turmeric

225 g/8 oz waxy potatoes,
  such as Maris Peer, cut into
  1-cm/½-inch cubes

3 shallots, finely chopped

1 bay leaf

½ tsp ground cumin

1 tsp finely grated fresh
  root ginger

¼ tsp chilli powder

4 tomatoes, roughly chopped

300 g/10½ oz fresh spinach
  de-stalked and roughly
  chopped

125 g/4½ oz fresh or
  frozen peas

1 tbsp lemon juice

salt and pepper

cooked basmati rice, to serve

1 Heat 2 tablespoons of the oil in a large frying pan or preheated wok. Add the turmeric and a pinch of salt, then carefully add the potatoes, stirring constantly to coat in the turmeric. Stir-fry for 5 minutes, remove from the pan and reserve.

2 Heat the remaining tablespoon of oil and stir-fry the shallots for 1–2 minutes. Mix in the bay leaf, cumin, ginger and chilli powder, then add the tomatoes and stir-fry for 2 minutes.

3 Add the spinach, mixing well to combine all the flavours. Cover and simmer for 2–3 minutes. Return the potatoes to the frying pan and add the peas and lemon juice. Cook for 5 minutes, or until the potatoes are tender.

4 Remove the frying pan from the heat, discard the bay leaf and season to taste with salt and pepper. Serve with cooked basmati rice.

" This is the quickest way I know to convince my friends that vegetarian food isn't boring. "

Rafi, Staines

main courses

Chilli con carne

4

We have certainly warmed to this Tex-Mex favourite that invariably brings out the cowboy in every city dude. Wonderfully versatile, you can serve it with tacos, rice, salad or even mashed potatoes. By the way, this tastes even better if you cook it the day before you are planning to eat it.

SERVES 4

Preparation time: 10 minutes
Cooking time: 1 hour

1 tbsp sunflower or corn oil

1 small onion, roughly chopped

1 or 2 garlic cloves, roughly chopped

1 green pepper, deseeded and diced

225 g/8 oz fresh beef mince

1 heaped tsp chilli powder

400 g/14 oz canned chopped tomatoes

½ tsp salt (optional)

400 g/14 oz canned kidney beans, drained and rinsed

SERVING SUGGESTIONS

grated cheese

shredded lettuce and tomatoes

Guacamole (see page 189)

fresh jalapeño chillies

freshly cooked rice or tortillas

1 Heat the oil in a shallow frying pan over a low heat. Stir in the onion, garlic and green pepper and cook gently for 5 minutes.

2 Add the beef mince and stir well. Increase the heat to high and cook for 5 minutes, stirring occasionally. Spoon off any excess fat. Sprinkle over the chilli powder and mix well. Continue cooking for 2–3 minutes. Stir in the tomatoes, reduce the heat, cover and cook gently for at least 30 minutes. You may need to add more tomatoes or a little water or beef stock if it starts to dry out.

3 Halfway through the cooking time check for seasoning and stir in the salt if needed. Add more chilli powder to taste, but be careful not to overdo it.

4 Add the drained kidney beans to the chilli mixture 10–15 minutes before the end of the cooking time so that they heat through with the meat and spices.

5 Serve with any of the accompaniments listed in the serving suggestions.

" This is a job for the boys. I cook a mean chilli and I'm teaching my son to make it too. **"** *Geoff, Hull*

main courses

Salmon steaks

The custom of serving fish with citrus fruit is given a new twist with this contemporary combination, served with lime salsa. It's a dish that wins in every way: healthy because of the omega oils, attractive because of the colours, affordable because of availability and, of course, simply scrumptious.

SERVES 4

Preparation time: 20 minutes
Marinating time: 1–2 hours
Cooking time: 7 minutes

grated rind and juice of 1 lime

1 large garlic clove, crushed

2 tbsp lemon-flavoured oil or
   extra virgin olive oil, plus
   extra for brushing

4 organic salmon steaks,
   such as Orkney, about
   175 g/6 oz each

fresh mint sprigs, to garnish

LIME SALSA

225 g/8 oz tomatoes

75 g/2¾ oz canned butter
   beans

1 fresh red chilli, deseeded and
   finely diced

2 spring onions, chopped

juice of 1 lime

1 tbsp chopped fresh mint

1 tbsp chopped fresh parsley

pinch of sugar

salt and pepper

1 Place the lime rind and juice in a large, shallow, non-metallic dish that will not react with acid (such as ceramic or glass). Add the garlic and oil and stir together well. Remove any bones from the fish, rinse the steaks under cold running water and pat dry with kitchen paper. Transfer to the dish and coat in the mixture. Cover with clingfilm and marinate in the refrigerator for 1–2 hours.

2 Meanwhile, to make the salsa, place the tomatoes in a heatproof bowl and cover with boiling water. Leave for 3–4 minutes, remove from the water and cool slightly. When cool enough to handle, pierce the skins with the point of a knife. Remove the skins, halve the tomatoes and remove the seeds. Chop the flesh and transfer to a mixing bowl. Mix in the remaining ingredients, cover with clingfilm and chill for 1 hour.

3 Preheat the grill to high, cover the grill rack with foil and brush with oil. Grill the fish for 7 minutes, turning once. Do not overcook. Garnish with mint sprigs and serve with the salsa.

COOK'S TIP
Although salmon is an oily fish, it is horribly easy to overcook and spoil. Keep a sharp eye on the steaks during grilling to prevent them from drying out.

" This dish is so good because it looks like you've gone to loads of trouble but it's really easy. "

Carole, Ayr

main courses

Basil & pine nut pesto

This lovely, aromatic sauce from Genoa (in the Liguria region of Italy) has certainly captured our imagination and enthusiasm. Often just tossed with pasta, it can be used in dozens of ways – here it complements and enlivens the sometimes rather bland flavour of chicken.

SERVES 4

Preparation time: 10 minutes
Cooking time: 10 minutes

PESTO

100 g/3½ oz shredded fresh basil

125 ml/4 fl oz extra virgin olive oil

3 tbsp pine kernels

3 garlic cloves, crushed

55 g/2 oz freshly grated Parmesan cheese

2 tbsp freshly grated pecorino cheese

2 tbsp vegetable oil

4 skinless, boneless chicken breasts

350 g/12 oz dried fettuccine

salt and pepper

sprig of fresh basil, to garnish

1 To make the pesto, place the basil, olive oil, pine kernels, garlic and a generous pinch of salt in a food processor or blender and process until smooth. Scrape the mixture into a bowl and stir in the cheeses.

2 Heat the vegetable oil in a frying pan over a medium heat. Fry the chicken breasts, turning once, for 8–10 minutes until the juices are no longer pink. Cut into small cubes.

3 Cook the pasta in plenty of boiling lightly salted water until al dente. Drain and transfer to a warmed serving dish. Add the chicken and pesto, then season with pepper. Toss well to mix.

4 Garnish with a basil sprig and serve warm.

COOK'S TIP
You can also make pesto the traditional way in a pestle and mortar. The result is slightly coarser and more rustic, which some people prefer. Place the basil, pine kernels, garlic and a large pinch of salt in a mortar and pound to a paste, then work in the grated Parmesan. Add the olive oil gradually, working it in with a wooden spoon until it is thoroughly incorporated and the sauce is creamy.

" This always makes me think of summer, no matter what the weather, and it cheers me up. "

Pam, Isle of Wight

"My favourite — reminds me of cuddling up with my boyfriend, watching a film, and scoffing the lot! *Nicci, Roath*

main courses

Pizza

As Italians migrated abroad and set up restaurants and pizzerias in cities as far apart as London and Sydney, they conquered the world with pizza. While all sorts of weird and wonderful toppings are on offer these days, nothing beats this classic combination of spinach and ricotta.

SERVES 2–4

Preparation time: 20 minutes
Rising time: 1 hour
Resting time: 15 minutes
Cooking time: 20–30 minutes

DOUGH

225 g/8 oz plain white flour, plus extra for dusting

225 g/8 oz wholemeal flour

1½ tsp salt

1 tsp easy-blend dried yeast

½ tsp sugar

300 ml/10 fl oz hand-hot water

2 tbsp olive oil, plus extra for oiling

TOPPING

2 tbsp olive oil, plus extra for drizzling

1 onion, thinly sliced

350 g/12 oz fresh spinach

6 tbsp ricotta cheese

½ tsp freshly grated nutmeg

2 tbsp pine kernels

115 g/4 oz fontina cheese, thinly sliced

salt and pepper

1 Sift both kinds of flour and the salt into a bowl and stir in the yeast and sugar. Make a well in the centre and add the water and oil. Using your fingers, gradually incorporate the flour into the liquid, then knead well on a work surface for at least 5 minutes until smooth and elastic. Shape the dough into a ball, return to the bowl, cover with oiled clingfilm and set aside in a warm place to rise for about 1 hour, or until doubled in size.

2 Turn the dough onto a lightly floured surface and knock back by punching gently with your fist. Divide in half then roll out each piece of dough into a 30-cm/12-inch round and place on oiled pizza pans or baking sheets. Push up the edges slightly. Cover with lightly oiled clingfilm and set aside to rest for 15 minutes.

3 Preheat the oven to 220°C/425°F/Gas Mark 7. Heat the oil in a saucepan. Add the onion and cook until softened, then add the spinach. Cook until wilted, then remove from the heat and reserve. Spread the ricotta cheese evenly over the pizza bases, then the onion mixture. Sprinkle with nutmeg and pine kernels and season to taste with salt and pepper. Top with the cheese and drizzle with oil. Bake for 20–30 minutes until sizzling.

COOK'S TIP

It is important to measure ingredients accurately when making a yeast dough, because if the proportions are wrong, it will not rise. It also helps if all the dough ingredients, apart from the water, are at room temperature and the mixing bowl has been warmed. The water should be hand-hot, that is, slightly warmer than lukewarm to activate the yeast. However, it should be no hotter or it will kill the yeast.

main courses

Cannelloni

This is a meal in itself, although you could serve it with salad if you like. Thick pasta tubes, here filled with marinated chicken, and baked in a delicious, creamy sauce are a welcome supper on a chilly winter's evening and also make a great weekend family lunch.

SERVES 4

Preparation time: 25 minutes
Marinating time: 30 minutes
Cooking time: 55 minutes
Standing time: 10 minutes

4 skinless, boneless chicken
  breasts, diced

2 tbsp olive oil

6 tbsp butter

500 ml/18 fl oz double cream

1 tsp salt

1 tsp pepper

¼ tsp freshly grated nutmeg

55 g/2 oz freshly grated
  Parmesan cheese

450 g/1 lb ricotta cheese

1 egg, lightly beaten

1 tbsp chopped fresh oregano

2 tbsp chopped fresh basil

225 g/8 oz dried cannelloni

75 g/2¾ oz mozzarella cheese,
  freshly grated

fresh basil sprigs, to garnish

MARINADE

125 ml/4 fl oz white wine
  vinegar

1 garlic clove, crushed

225 ml/8 fl oz olive oil

1 To make the marinade, mix the vinegar, garlic and olive oil together in a large bowl. Add the chicken, cover with clingfilm and leave to marinate for 30 minutes.

2 Heat the 2 tablespoons of olive oil in a frying pan. Drain the chicken and cook 2–7 minutes, stirring, until no longer pink. Reserve.

3 Melt the butter in a saucepan over a medium–high heat. Add the cream, salt, pepper and nutmeg. Stir until thickened. Reduce the heat, add the Parmesan cheese and stir until melted. Remove from the heat.

4 Heat the oven to 180°C/350°F/Gas Mark 4. Mix the ricotta, egg and herbs together in a large bowl. Stir in the chicken then remove from the heat. Stuff the cannelloni with the chicken mixture. Pour half the sauce into a 23 x 33-cm/ 9 x 13-inch baking dish. Place the stuffed cannelloni on top. Pour over the remaining sauce. Sprinkle with the mozzarella and cover with foil. Bake in the preheated oven for 45 minutes. Leave the dish to stand for 10 minutes before garnishing with basil sprigs and serving.

COOK'S TIP

Stuffing cannelloni tubes is quite a fiddly process. You can use the handle of a teaspoon to push the chicken mixture into the middle of the tubes. Some cooks recommend using a piping bag fitted with a large, plain nozzle. However, in this instance, the chicken is likely to cause a blockage, unless it is very finely diced.

main courses

Fettuccine all' alfredo

Three cheers for Alfredo and the classic simplicity of this superb combination of ribbon pasta, cream, butter and Parmesan cheese. For best results and an authentic flavour, always grate the Parmesan freshly from a block. It will keep in the refrigerator for ages.

SERVES 4

Preparation time: 5 minutes
Cooking time: 5 minutes

25 g/1 oz butter

200 ml/7 fl oz double cream

450 g/1 lb fresh fettuccine

1 tbsp olive oil

90 g/3¼ oz freshly grated
  Parmesan cheese, plus extra
  to serve

pinch of freshly grated nutmeg

salt and pepper

fresh parsley sprigs, to garnish

VARIATION

This classic Roman dish is often served with the addition of strips of ham and fresh peas. Add 225 g/ 8 oz shelled cooked peas and 175 g/6 oz ham strips with the Parmesan cheese in step 4.

1 Place the butter and 150 ml/ 5 fl oz of the cream in a large saucepan and bring the mixture to the boil over a medium heat. Reduce the heat and simmer gently for about 1½ minutes, or until slightly thickened.

2 Meanwhile, bring a large saucepan of lightly salted water to the boil. Add the fettuccine and oil, return to the boil and cook for 2–3 minutes until al dente. Drain the fettuccine thoroughly, return it to the saucepan and pour the sauce over it.

3 Return the saucepan to a low heat and toss the fettuccine in the sauce until coated.

4 Add the remaining cream, the Parmesan cheese and nutmeg to the fettuccine mixture and season to taste with salt and pepper. Toss thoroughly to coat while gently heating through.

5 Transfer the fettuccine mixture to a warmed serving plate and garnish with parsley sprigs. Serve immediately, adding extra grated Parmesan cheese separately.

" Never mind the wheel, pasta was Man's greatest invention and this is the best way to serve it. "

Luke, Hove

main courses

Pasta provençal

10

This colourful **pasta salad** is packed with glorious Mediterranean vegetables and then tossed in a flavoursome low-fat dressing — so there's no good reason why you shouldn't have a second helping. Much more fun than boring old lettuce, this is a perfect summer dish.

SERVES 4

Preparation time: 10 minutes
Cooking time: 10 minutes

225 g/8 oz dried penne

1 tbsp olive oil

25 g/1 oz stoned black olives, drained and chopped

25 g/1 oz dry-pack sun-dried tomatoes, soaked, drained and chopped

400 g/14 oz canned artichoke hearts, drained and halved

115 g/4 oz baby courgettes, trimmed and sliced

115 g/4 oz baby plum tomatoes, halved

100 g/3½ oz assorted baby salad leaves

salt and pepper

shredded basil leaves, to garnish

DRESSING

4 tbsp passata

2 tbsp low-fat natural fromage frais

1 tbsp unsweetened orange juice

1 small bunch of fresh basil, shredded

1 Cook the penne according to the packet instructions. Do not overcook the pasta – it should still have 'bite'. Drain well and return to the saucepan. Stir in the oil, salt and pepper, olives and sun-dried tomatoes. Leave to cool.

2 Gently mix the artichokes, courgettes and plum tomatoes into the cooked pasta.

3 Arrange the salad leaves in a large serving bowl.

4 To make the dressing, mix all the ingredients together and toss into the vegetables and pasta.

5 Spoon the mixture on top of the salad leaves and garnish with shredded basil leaves.

COOK'S TIP

Basil is a delicate herb, so it is often best to shred or tear it with your fingers. Using a knife can bruise the leaves, which will then turn black at the edges and spoil the appearance of the dish.

" It says something when it's always the first sale on the cake stall at the school fête. "

Val, Carlisle

desserts

Carrot cake

A knockout winner with everybody, this easy-to-bake dessert cake is irresistible, as popular with kids as it is with adults. Light as air in texture, it makes the most of the natural sweetness of carrots and looks so tempting with a simple icing and walnut decoration.

SERVES 6

Preparation time: 25 minutes
Cooking time: 55 minutes
Cooling time: 1 hour

butter, for greasing

100 g/3½ oz self-raising flour

pinch of salt

1 tsp ground mixed spice

½ tsp ground nutmeg

125 g/4½ oz soft brown sugar

2 eggs, beaten

5 tbsp sunflower oil

125 g/4½ oz carrots, grated

1 banana, chopped

25 g/1 oz chopped, toasted
  mixed nuts

ICING

40 g/1½ oz butter, softened

3 tbsp cream cheese

175 g/6 oz icing sugar, sifted

1 tsp orange juice

grated rind of ½ orange

walnut halves or pieces, to
  decorate

1 Preheat the oven to 190°C/375°F/Gas Mark 5. Grease an 18-cm/7-inch square cake tin with butter and line with baking paper.

2 Sift the flour, salt, mixed spice and nutmeg into a bowl. Stir in the brown sugar, then stir in the eggs and oil. Add the carrots, banana and chopped mixed nuts and mix together well.

3 Spoon the mixture into the prepared cake tin and level the surface. Transfer the cake to the preheated oven and bake for 55 minutes, or until golden and just firm to the touch. Remove from the oven and leave to cool. When cool enough to handle, turn the cake out onto a wire rack and leave it to cool completely.

4 To make the icing, place the butter, cream cheese, icing sugar, and orange juice and rind into a bowl and beat together until creamy. Spread the icing over the top of the cold cake, then use a fork to make shallow wavy lines in the icing. Scatter over the walnuts, cut the cake into bars and serve.

desserts

Fresh fruit salad

Simply perfect and perfectly simple, this is the ideal dessert to end a relaxed alfresco lunch or supper on a hot summer's day. Luscious and refreshing, colourful and pretty, healthy and revitalizing, effortless and economical — no wonder it scored highly.

SERVES 4

Preparation time: 20 minutes
Cooking time: 3 minutes
Chilling time: 1 hour

6 tbsp caster sugar

400 ml/14 fl oz water

½ tsp ground mixed spice

grated rind of ½ lemon

1 pawpaw

1 mango

1 pineapple

4 oranges, peeled and cut
into segments

125 g/4½ oz strawberries,
hulled and quartered

single or double cream, to
serve (optional)

1 Place the sugar, water, mixed spice, and lemon rind in a saucepan. Bring to the boil, stirring constantly, then continue to boil for 1 minute. Remove from the heat and leave to cool to room temperature. Transfer to a jug or bowl, cover with clingfilm and chill in the refrigerator for at least 1 hour.

2 Peel and halve the pawpaw and remove the seeds. Cut the flesh into small chunks or slices, and place in a large bowl. Cut the mango either side lengthways, close to the stone. Remove and discard the stone. Peel and cut the flesh into small chunks or slices, and add to the bowl. Cut off the top and bottom of the pineapple and remove the hard skin. Cut the pineapple in half lengthways, then into quarters, and remove the tough core. Cut the remaining flesh into small pieces and add to the bowl. Add the orange segments and strawberries. Pour over the chilled syrup, cover with clingfilm and chill until required.

3 Remove the fruit salad from the refrigerator and serve with single or double cream, if using.

"My kids don't need persuading to eat fruit. They literally beg me to make fruit salad."

Toni, Maidenhead

Somehow a meal never seems complete without a proper dessert and this is one of our family's favourites. *Maggie, Exeter*

desserts

Baked apples

It's the red wine that makes our most popular fruit blush, not modesty at its widespread acclaim. This delicious recipe gives an old favourite a sophisticated twist, as the apples are filled with a warmly spiced mixture of fresh and dried fruit before baking.

SERVES 4

Preparation time: 15 minutes
Cooking time: 40–45 minutes

4 medium cooking apples

1 tbsp lemon juice

50 g/1¾ oz blueberries

50 g/1¾ oz raisins

25 g/1 oz chopped, toasted
  mixed nuts

½ tsp ground cinnamon

2 tbsp soft brown sugar

275 ml/9½ fl oz red wine

2 tsp cornflour

4 tsp water

double cream, to serve

1 Preheat the oven to 200°C/400°F/Gas Mark 6. Using a sharp knife, score a line around the centre of each apple. Core the apples, then brush the centres with the lemon juice to prevent discolouration. Transfer them to a small roasting tin.

2 Place the blueberries and raisins in a bowl, then add the nuts, cinnamon and sugar. Mix together well. Pile the mixture into the centre of each apple, then pour over the wine.

3 Transfer the stuffed apples to the preheated oven and bake for 40–45 minutes, or until tender. Remove from the oven, then lift the apples out of the oven and keep them warm.

4 Blend the cornflour with the water, then add the mixture to the cooking juices in the roasting tin. Transfer to the hob and cook over a medium heat, stirring, until thickened. Remove from the heat and pour over the apples. Serve the apples with double cream.

VARIATION

This is also a great way to cook stone fruits, such as peaches and nectarines. Halve and stone them, then hollow out the cavities a little more with the point of a knife. Fill the cavities with the fruit and nut mixture, pour over the wine and bake as described in the recipe for 30–35 minutes.

"It makes me
really happy to
see them all round
the kitchen table
at supper times.
I think good food
makes good
families."

Sandra, Derby

Chapter four

FRIDAY NIGHT SPECIALS

The hot choice for light meals is nachos, here served with a fiery salsa, while the gold medal for main meals goes to succulent braised duck. When it comes to desserts, our allegiance is to chocolate with a melt-in-the-mouth cheesecake in first place.

light meals

Nachos

A scorching victory for nachos, here served with a fast and fiery Mexican dip. You could also serve alone with other dippers, such as raw vegetables, or spoon it onto burgers and steaks - sparingly, unless you're very brave.

SERVES 4

Preparation time: 5 minutes
Cooking time: 5–10 minutes

2 packets of nachos or tortilla chips

4 tbsp fresh jalapeño chillies, finely sliced

115 g/4 oz Cheddar cheese, grated

2 tbsp finely chopped fresh coriander, to garnish

TO SERVE

tomato salsa

Guacamole (see page 189)

soured cream

1 Preheat the oven to 190°C/375°F/Gas Mark 5.

2 Tip the nachos into a shallow ovenproof dish. Scatter over the chillies and top with the cheese. Bake in the preheated oven for 5–10 minutes to melt the cheese.

3 Remove the nachos from the oven, garnish with coriander and serve with salsa, Guacamole and a dish of soured cream.

COOK'S TIP

For a speedy tomato salsa, peel 450 g/1 lb tomatoes, either by plunging them into boiling water for 1 minute or by holding them in a gas flame on the end of a skewer. Halve them and scoop out the seeds, then dice the flesh and place in a bowl. Stir in the juice of 1 lime, 3 tbsp chopped fresh coriander, 1 finely chopped garlic clove and Tabasco sauce to taste. Season with salt and pepper, cover and store in the refrigerator until required.

" Nachos - perfect for naughty nights! "

Claire, London

light meals

Spring rolls

A seasoned filling of thinly sliced vegetables and beansprouts encased in pastry and deep-fried to crisp perfection at the table is just so easy to eat. Served with soy or chilli sauce for dipping, they're incredibly more-ish — ideal food to unwind with.

SERVES 4

Preparation time: 20 minutes
Cooking time: 15–20 minutes

2 tbsp chilli oil

4 spring onions, finely chopped

1 red pepper, deseeded and
   finely sliced into 5-cm/2-inch
   lengths

1 carrot, finely sliced into
   5-cm/2-inch lengths

85 g/3 oz beansprouts

1 tbsp lemon juice

1 tsp soy sauce

8 sheets filo pastry, halved

2 tbsp butter, melted

1 egg white, slightly beaten

1 litre/1¾ pints groundnut oil

salt and pepper

soy or chilli sauce, to serve

1 Heat the chilli oil in a preheated wok or large frying pan. Add the spring onions, red pepper and carrot and stir-fry for 2 minutes. Add the beansprouts, lemon juice and soy sauce and stir-fry for 1 minute, then add salt and pepper to taste and remove from the heat.

2 Spread out the pastry on a clean work surface and brush with melted butter. Spoon a little of the vegetable mixture onto one short end of each sheet of pastry, fold in the long sides and roll up to enclose the filling. Brush the edges with egg white to seal.

3 Pour the groundnut oil into a metal fondue pot (it should be no more than one-third full). Heat on the hob to 190°C/375°F, or until a cube of bread browns in 30 seconds. Using protective gloves, transfer the fondue pot to a lit tabletop burner. To serve, allow your guests to spear the spring rolls onto fondue forks and dip into the hot oil until cooked to taste (the spring rolls will need 2–3 minutes). Drain off the excess oil. Serve with the soy or chilli sauce.

VARIATION
For a non-vegetarian version of this dish, you can add diced cooked pork, chicken or cooked peeled prawns to the filling.

COOK'S TIP
If you would prefer to use spring roll wrappers, you can buy them at Chinese food shops. Wheat flour wrappers are usually sold frozen and must be thawed and separated before use. Rice flour wrappers need to be soaked before filling.

light meals

Onion bhajis

Biting into the crisp batter to taste the soft, spicy onion filling is pure pleasure, so it's not really a surprise that these classic Indian snacks attracted so many votes. You can serve them as the first course of an Indian — or, for that matter, Western — meal too.

SERVES 4

Preparation time: 20 minutes
Standing time: 30 minutes
Cooking time: 15–20 minutes

200 g/7 oz gram flour

1 egg, beaten

240 ml/8 ½ fl oz cold water

1 tsp ground turmeric

1 tsp chilli powder

1 tsp ground coriander

1 tsp ground cumin

2 large onions, chopped

1 garlic clove, chopped

1 tbsp chopped fresh coriander

vegetable oil, for frying

naan bread, to serve

MINT RAITA

225 ml/8 fl oz natural yogurt

1½ tbsp water

1 tsp mint sauce

1 small onion, very finely
  chopped

salt

fresh mint leaves, to garnish

1 Place the flour in a large bowl and mix in the egg. Gradually mix in enough of the water to make a smooth, thick batter. Stir in the turmeric, chilli powder, ground coriander and cumin. Cover with clingfilm and leave to stand for 20 minutes.

2 Meanwhile, make the raita. Pour the yogurt into a bowl and whisk gently until smooth, then whisk in the water. Whisk in the mint sauce and onion until thoroughly combined and season to taste with salt. Cover with clingfilm and chill in the refrigerator until ready to serve.

3 Remove the clingfilm from the batter and stir in the onions, garlic and fresh coriander. Mix well, replace the clingfilm and leave to stand for a further 10 minutes.

4 Heat 2.5 cm/1 inch of oil in a large frying pan to 190°C/375°F, or until a cube of bread browns in 30 seconds. Drop a tablespoonful of the batter into the hot oil and cook, turning, until golden. Lift out with a slotted spoon and drain on kitchen paper. Cook the remaining bhajis in batches and drain on kitchen paper.

5 Remove the raita from the refrigerator and garnish with mint leaves. Serve the bhajis with naan bread and the raita.

COOK'S TIP

As an alternative or addition to the mint raita, you could serve a slightly spicy, herb sauce. Place 2 bunches of roughly chopped fresh coriander in a food processor with 25 g/1 oz roughly chopped peanuts, 1 deseeded and roughly chopped fresh green chilli, 1 tbsp lime juice, 1 roughly chopped garlic clove, 1 tsp sugar, 1 tsp salt and 125 ml/4 fl oz water. Process until smooth, then scrape into a bowl, cover and store in the refrigerator until required.

" Onion bhajis finish off a Friday night — a man or an onion bhaji with yogurt sauce? The Onion bhaji wins every time! "

Kirsty, Manchester

light meals

Egg fried rice

SERVES 4

Preparation time: 5 minutes
Cooking time: 15–20 minutes

150 g/5½ oz long-grain rice

3 eggs, beaten

2 tbsp vegetable oil

2 garlic cloves, crushed

4 spring onions, chopped

125 g/4½ oz cooked peas

1 tbsp light soy sauce

pinch of salt

shredded spring onion,
  to garnish

VARIATION

You could add prawns, ham or chicken in step 3, if you wish.

COOK'S TIP

The rice is rinsed under cold running water to wash out the starch and prevent it from sticking together.

A heavy week? Too tired to cook much? Too tired to eat much? This simple, tasty and nutritious combination is sure to hit the spot. It's versatile too as you can add other ingredients according to taste and what you have in the refrigerator. It also makes a great accompaniment to other Chinese dishes.

1 Cook the rice in a saucepan of boiling water for 10–12 minutes until almost cooked, but not soft. Drain well, rinse under cold running water and drain thoroughly.

2 Place the beaten eggs in a saucepan and cook over a low heat, stirring constantly until softly scrambled. Remove the saucepan from the heat and reserve.

3 Preheat a wok over a medium heat. Add the oil and swirl it around to coat the sides of the wok. When the oil is hot, add the garlic, spring onions and peas and sauté, stirring occasionally, for 1–2 minutes.

4 Stir the rice into the mixture in the wok, mixing to combine.

5 Add the eggs, soy sauce and salt to the wok and stir to mix the egg in thoroughly.

6 Transfer to serving dishes and serve garnished with the shredded spring onion.

" What I love about Chinese food is it's so quick but tastes great. "
Sam, Battersea

light meals

Vegetable samosas

Another classic Indian snack, these crisp, little pastry parcels of aromatically spiced vegetables must be as popular here as they are on the many stalls that line the streets of India's cities. They're terrific for Friday nights as you can prepare them in advance and then cook in minutes.

SERVES 4

Preparation time: 25 minutes
Cooling time: 15 minutes
Cooking time: 25–30 minutes

FILLING

1 carrot, diced

200 g/7 oz sweet potato, diced

85 g/3 oz frozen peas

2 tbsp ghee or vegetable oil

1 onion, chopped

1 garlic clove, chopped

2.5-cm/1-inch piece fresh root
  ginger, grated

1 tsp ground turmeric

1 tsp ground cumin

½ tsp chilli powder

½ tsp garam masala

1 tsp lime juice

vegetable oil, for frying

salt and pepper

PASTRY

150 g/5½ oz plain flour,
  plus extra for dusting

3 tbsp butter, diced

4 tbsp warm milk

TO SERVE

lime wedges

mango chutney (see below)

1 Bring a saucepan of water to the boil, add the carrot and cook for 4 minutes. Add the sweet potato and cook for 4 minutes, then add the peas and cook for 3 minutes. Drain. Heat the ghee in a clean saucepan over a medium heat, add the onion, garlic, ginger, spices and lime juice and cook, stirring, for 3 minutes. Add the vegetables and season. Cook, stirring, for 2 minutes. Remove from the heat, leave to cool slightly, then mash.

ACCOMPANIMENTS

Although ready-made chutney is widely available, the home-made version is more delicious. Peel, halve and stone 1 kg/2 lb 4 oz mangoes. Dice the flesh and place in a large bowl. Add 600 ml/1 pint water and 4 tbsp salt, cover and leave to soak overnight. The next day, drain and discard the liquid. Gently heat 450 ml/16 fl oz vinegar with 450 g/1 lb sugar in a large saucepan, stirring until the sugar has dissolved. When the mixture has come to the boil, add the mangoes, a few at a time, stirring to coat well. Stir in 85 g/3 oz raisins, 85 g/3 oz dried and stoned dates, 2 tsp chopped fresh root ginger, 2 tsp crushed garlic, 2 tsp chilli powder and 1 cinnamon stick. Return the mixture to the boil, then reduce the heat and simmer for 1 hour until thickened. Remove from the heat and leave to cool completely before removing the cinnamon stick and ladling into a clean jar. Seal and store in a cool, dark, dry place until required.

2 Place the flour in a bowl and rub in the butter. Add the milk and mix to form a dough. Knead briefly and divide into 4. Roll into balls on a lightly floured work surface, then roll out into rounds 17 cm/6½ inches in diameter. Cut the rounds in half. Place a little of the filling on one side of each half round, brush the edges of the dough with water, then fold over into triangles and seal the edges.

3 Heat 2.5 cm/1 inch of oil in a frying pan to 180–190°C/350–375°F, or until a cube of bread browns in 30 seconds. Cook the samosas in batches for 3–4 minutes, or until golden. Drain on kitchen paper and serve with lime wedges and mango chutney.

main courses

Chinese crispy duck

Given that the chefs of northern China have spent generations perfecting the art of combining flavours and are rightly proud of their duck dishes, this is a deserving winner among the main course recipes. While perhaps not so famous as Peking duck, this braised duck is a lot easier to make.

SERVES 4

Preparation time: 20 minutes
Cooking time: 2 hours

3 tbsp soy sauce

¼ tsp Chinese five-spice powder

¼ tsp pepper and pinch of salt

4 duck legs or breasts, cut into
   pieces

3 tbsp vegetable oil

I tsp dark sesame oil

I tsp finely chopped root ginger

I large garlic clove, finely
   chopped

4 spring onions, white part
   thickly sliced, green part
   shredded

2 tbsp rice wine or dry sherry

I tbsp oyster sauce

3 whole star anise

2 tsp black peppercorns

450–600 ml/16 fl oz–I pint
   chicken stock or water

6 dried shiitake mushrooms,
   soaked in warm water for
   20 minutes

225 g/8 oz canned water
   chestnuts, drained

2 tbsp cornflour

1 Combine I tablespoon of the soy sauce, the five-spice powder, pepper and salt and rub over the duck pieces. Place 2½ tablespoons of vegetable oil in a heatproof casserole, add the duck pieces and cook until browned, then transfer to a plate and reserve.

2 Drain the fat from the casserole and wipe out. Heat the sesame oil and remaining vegetable oil in it. Add the ginger and garlic. Cook for a few seconds. Add the white spring onion. Cook for a few seconds. Return the duck to the casserole. Add the rice wine, oyster sauce, star anise, peppercorns and remaining soy sauce. Pour in enough stock to just cover the duck. Bring to the boil, cover and simmer gently for I ½ hours, adding more stock if necessary.

3 Drain the mushrooms and squeeze dry. Slice the caps and add to the duck with the water chestnuts. Simmer for a further 20 minutes.

4 Mix the cornflour with 2 tablespoons of the cooking liquid to form a smooth paste. Add to the remaining liquid, stirring, until thickened. Garnish with the green spring onion shreds before serving.

main courses

Korma

With its characteristic creamy texture and rich flavour, this Indian vegetarian curry is ideal for those who like milder spices and a warming, subtle taste. Like many Indian curries, it's just as popular with meat-eaters as it is with vegetarians, though it can be made with meat or seafood.

SERVES 4

Preparation time: 15 minutes
Cooking time: 40–45 minutes

4 tbsp ghee or vegetable oil

2 onions, chopped

2 garlic cloves, chopped

I fresh red chilli, chopped

I tbsp grated fresh root ginger

2 tomatoes, peeled and
  chopped

I orange pepper, deseeded and
  cut into small pieces

I large potato, cut into chunks

200 g/7 oz cauliflower florets

½ tsp salt

I tsp ground turmeric

I tsp ground cumin

I tsp ground coriander

I tsp garam masala

200 ml/7 fl oz vegetable stock
  or water

150 ml/5 fl oz natural yogurt

150 ml/5 fl oz single cream

25 g/I oz fresh coriander,
  chopped

freshly cooked rice, to serve

1 Heat the ghee in a large saucepan over a medium heat, add the onions and garlic and cook, stirring, for 3 minutes. Add the chilli and ginger and cook for a further 4 minutes. Add the tomatoes, pepper, potato, cauliflower, salt and spices and cook, stirring, for a further 3 minutes. Stir in the stock and bring to the boil. Reduce the heat and simmer for 25 minutes.

2 Stir in the yogurt and cream and cook, stirring, for a further 5 minutes. Add the fresh coriander and heat through.

3 Serve the curry with freshly cooked rice.

"I fell in love with my husband over Korma, which to me tastes like falling in love – he knows his luck's in if the sweet smell of Korma greets him when he comes home!"

Kate, Deal

main courses

Chicken tikka masala

Famously once described as 'Britain's national dish' by a former government minister, this was destined to attract a high percentage of votes, regardless of any individual's political affiliations. Serve it with salad and naan as a main course or on its own as a starter.

SERVES 4

Preparation time: 15 minutes
Marinating time: 2–8 hours
Cooking time: 15 minutes

450 g/1 lb skinless, boneless
   chicken breasts, cut into
   bite-sized chunks
1 tsp salt
5 tbsp lemon juice
4–6 tbsp single cream
fresh coriander sprigs,
   to garnish

MARINADE
1 large garlic clove, finely
   chopped
½ onion, grated
1 tbsp desiccated coconut
1 tsp ground cumin
1½ tsp chilli powder
1 tsp garam masala
1 tsp ground turmeric
1 tsp paprika
1 tsp ground coriander
2 tsp chopped fresh coriander
100 ml/3½ fl oz natural yogurt
freshly ground black pepper,
   to taste

TO SERVE
lemon wedges
basmati rice
naan bread or chapatis

1 Place the chicken, salt and lemon juice in a non-metallic bowl and mix well. Mix all the marinade ingredients together in a separate bowl, then add to the chicken and stir gently to combine. Cover with clingfilm and leave to marinate in the refrigerator for at least 2 hours, or preferably overnight.

2 When ready to cook, preheat the grill or barbecue. Remove the chicken from the refrigerator and thread onto metal skewers. Baste with some of the marinade. Cook under the hot grill, or over hot coals for 15 minutes, turning and basting the chicken frequently with the remaining marinade.

3 Remove the chicken skewers from the heat, transfer to a serving platter and pour over the cream. Garnish with coriander sprigs and serve with lemon wedges, accompanied by basmati rice and naan bread or chapatis.

" I've eaten Chicken tikka masala every Friday night for ages – and couldn't live without it! "
Tracey, Manchester

main courses

Sweet & sour pork 4

This is a terrific dish for a Friday night get-together as once you've made the quick and easy stuffing, all you have to do is pop the meat in the oven and leave it to cook in its delicious Chinese-style sauce. Then you can put your feet up and talk to your guests.

SERVES 4

Preparation time: 15 minutes
Cooking time: 1¾ hours
Standing time: 15 minutes

1 kg/2 lb 4 oz pork loin,
  backbone removed and
  rind scored
6 tbsp clear honey
1 tbsp wine vinegar
1 tsp soy sauce
1 tsp Dijon mustard
salt and pepper
fresh sage leaves, to garnish

STUFFING
6 tbsp butter
1 onion, chopped
100 g/3½ oz white mushrooms,
  chopped
100 g/3½ oz fresh breadcrumbs
2 tbsp finely chopped fresh sage
1 tbsp lemon juice

TO SERVE
roast potatoes
roasted root vegetables

1 Preheat the oven to 230°C/450°F/Gas Mark 8. To make the stuffing, melt the butter in a saucepan over a medium heat. Add the onion and cook, stirring, for about 3 minutes until softened. Add the mushrooms and cook for a further 2 minutes. Remove from the heat and stir in the breadcrumbs, sage, lemon juice and seasoning.

2 Place the stuffing in the middle of the pork loin, then roll up and tie the loin with several pieces of string. Place the joint in a roasting tin, rub the skin with plenty of salt and season with pepper. Mix the honey, vinegar, soy sauce and mustard together in a small bowl. Pour the mixture over the pork.

3 Cook in the preheated oven for 20 minutes, then reduce the oven temperature to 180°C/350°F/ Gas Mark 4 and cook, basting occasionally, for 1¼ hours, or until cooked through. Remove from the oven and leave for 15 minutes.

4 Garnish the pork with fresh sage leaves and serve with roast potatoes and roasted root vegetables.

" This is terrific for Fridays because it tastes so special but isn't hard to do – just what you want for the weekend. **"** *Ros, Loughborough*

"Eating fish and chips out of newspaper, when my husband and I were courting over 35 years ago."

Barbara, Wrexham

main courses

Fish & chips

There is absolutely no way that this could have been left out – but this ever-popular traditional dish has moved on from British bulldog to cool Britannia. No longer a Friday fry-up, this is a healthier version that loses none of the flavour and crispness of the original.

SERVES 4

Preparation time: 15 minutes
Cooking time: 40–45 minutes

450 g/1 lb floury potatoes, such as King Edward or Maris Piper, peeled and cut into thick, even-sized chips
vegetable oil spray
55 g/2 oz plain white flour
1 egg
55 g/2 oz fresh white breadcrumbs, seasoned with salt and pepper
4 cod or haddock fillets

TO SERVE
4 lemon wedges
fresh parsley sprigs

1 Preheat the oven to 200°C/400°F/Gas Mark 6. Line 2 baking sheets with non-stick liner.

2 Rinse the chipped potatoes under cold running water, then dry well on a clean tea towel. Place in a bowl, spray with oil and toss together until coated. Spread the chips on a baking sheet and cook in the preheated oven for 40–45 minutes, turning once, until golden.

3 Meanwhile, place the flour on a plate, beat the egg in a shallow dish and spread the seasoned breadcrumbs on a large plate. Dip the fish fillets in the flour to coat, then in the egg, allowing any excess to drip off, and finally in the breadcrumbs, patting them firmly into the fish. Place the fish in a single layer on the other baking sheet.

4 Fifteen minutes before the chips have cooked, bake the fish fillets in the oven for 10–15 minutes, turning them once during cooking, until tender. Place the fish on individual plates, garnish with lemon wedges and parsley sprigs and serve with the chips.

ACCOMPANIMENTS
For a quick and easy tartare sauce, mix 300 ml/10 fl oz mayonnaise, 2 tbsp chopped capers, 2 tbsp chopped gherkins, 2 finely chopped spring onions and 1 tbsp chopped fresh parsley together. You can use salted or preserved capers depending on which you prefer. However, rub off any salt with your fingers and rinse capers that have been preserved in vinegar or brine.

main courses

Pizza

Arguably the great grandfather and progenitor of all pizzas, this version is clearly still one of the best and most loved — for Brits as well as Italians. The trick is to use good-quality mozzarella cheese, preferably mozzarella di bufala, made from buffalo's milk.

SERVES 4

Preparation time: 10 minutes
Cooking time: 50–55 minutes

2 red onions

3 tbsp olive oil

2 garlic cloves, chopped

400 g/14 oz canned chopped
  tomatoes

1 tbsp chopped fresh oregano

1 tsp dried mixed herbs

1 bay leaf

2½ tbsp tomato purée

½ tsp sugar

1 tsp butter

200 g/7 oz white mushrooms,
  sliced

1 tbsp plain flour, for dusting

2 ready-prepared pizza bases,
  about 23 cm/9 inches in
  diameter

300 g/10½ oz mozzarella
  cheese, chopped

4 tomatoes, sliced

1 red pepper, deseeded and cut
  into thin strips

salt and pepper

fresh basil leaves, to garnish

1 Chop 1 onion, slice the other, and reserve. Heat 1½ tablespoons of the oil in a large saucepan. Add one of the garlic cloves and the chopped onion (reserve the sliced onion) and cook, stirring, over a medium heat for 3 minutes. Add the canned tomatoes and the herbs, tomato purée and sugar. Season and bring to the boil, stirring. Reduce the heat and simmer, uncovered, for 15 minutes.

2 Preheat the oven to 190°C/375°F/Gas Mark 5. Melt the butter in a saucepan over a medium heat. Add the mushrooms and cook, stirring, for 5 minutes, then remove from the heat and drain. Remove the tomato sauce from the heat and discard the bay leaf.

3 Lightly flour 2 baking sheets and place a pizza base on each one. Spread tomato sauce over each base. Scatter over the mozzarella, remaining garlic and sliced onion. Arrange the mushrooms, fresh tomatoes and red pepper over the top and drizzle over the remaining oil. Bake in the preheated oven for 20–25 minutes. Remove from the oven and garnish with basil leaves before serving.

COOK'S TIP

For speedy, home-made pizza bases, sift together 350 g/12 oz self-raising flour and 1 tsp salt into a bowl. Add 55 g/2 oz butter and rub it in with your fingertips. Stir in 175–225 ml/6–8 fl oz milk and mix to a soft dough. Turn out onto a lightly floured surface, knead gently, then halve and shape into 2 rounds.

❝ Memories of my Italian grandparents cooking, laughing and arguing in a huge kitchen that we all seemed to live in. It always smelt lovely and felt warm and welcoming; all my friends used to love to come round... you always got fed! ❞

Rowena, Balblair

main courses

Chicken chow mein

7

Quick, easy and packed with flavour, this stir-fried noodle dish is one of China's best known and best loved. Chicken is the favourite, but the recipe can be easily adapted with pork, prawns or a mixture of meat and seafood. It's a great pick-me-up if you're suffering from Friday fatigue.

SERVES 4

Preparation time: 10 minutes
Cooking time: 10–12 minutes

250 g/9 oz packet medium
  egg noodles

2 tbsp sunflower oil

275 g/9¾ oz cooked chicken
  breasts, shredded

1 garlic clove, finely chopped

1 red pepper, deseeded and
  thinly sliced

100 g/3½ oz shiitake
  mushrooms, sliced

6 spring onions, sliced

100 g/3½ oz beansprouts

3 tbsp soy sauce

1 tbsp sesame oil

VARIATION
You can make the chow mein with a selection of vegetables to create a vegetarian dish, if you prefer.

1 Place the egg noodles in a large bowl or dish and break them up slightly.

2 Pour enough boiling water over the noodles to cover and leave to stand while preparing the other ingredients.

3 Preheat a wok over a medium heat. Add the sunflower oil and swirl it around to coat the sides of the wok. When the oil is hot, add the shredded chicken, garlic, pepper, mushrooms, spring onions and beansprouts to the wok and stir-fry for about 5 minutes.

4 Drain the noodles thoroughly then add them to the wok, toss well and stir-fry for a further 5 minutes.

5 Drizzle the soy sauce and sesame oil over the chow mein and toss until well combined.

6 Transfer the chicken chow mein to warmed serving bowls and serve immediately.

"" This just goes to show that happiness is a hot wok. ""

Kim, Reigate

main courses

Chicken jalfrezi

This stir-fried curry, richly flavoured with peppers, onions and spices, transforms chicken, which can otherwise be rather boring, into something really special. Just serve it with naan bread and mango chutney to make a meal that is fit for a rajah.

SERVES 4

Preparation time: 25 minutes
Cooling time: 15 minutes
Cooking time: 40–45 minutes

1 red pepper, quartered and
   deseeded

1 green pepper, quartered
   and deseeded

3 tbsp ghee or butter

1 tbsp chilli oil

1 large onion, finely chopped

3 large garlic cloves, crushed

2.5-cm/1-inch piece fresh root
   ginger, grated

1 tsp chilli powder

1 tsp ground turmeric

1 tsp ground cumin

1 tsp ground coriander

1 tsp garam masala

4 skinless, boneless chicken
   breasts, cut into bite-sized
   chunks

75 g/2¾ oz unsalted cashew
   nuts, halved

100 ml/3½ fl oz natural yogurt

3 large tomatoes, peeled and
   chopped

1 tbsp tomato purée

100 ml/3½ fl oz boiling water

TO SERVE

naan bread

mango chutney (see page 151)

1 Preheat the grill to medium. Flatten the peppers, then place skin-side up on a grill pan. Cook under the hot grill for 10 minutes, turning frequently, until blackened and blistered all over. Transfer to a polythene bag and leave until cool. Peel off the skins and chop the flesh.

2 Heat the ghee and oil in a large saucepan over a medium heat. Add the onion, garlic and ginger and cook, stirring, for 4 minutes, or until softened and golden. Add the chilli powder, turmeric, cumin, coriander and garam masala and cook, stirring, for 1 minute. Add the chicken and cashew nuts and cook, stirring, for 5 minutes.

3 Remove from the heat and stir in the yogurt. Return to the heat and stir in the tomatoes, tomato purée, peppers and boiling water. Bring to the boil, then reduce the heat and simmer, stirring frequently, for 20–25 minutes, or until the sauce has thickened.

4 Serve immediately with naan bread and mango chutney.

COOK'S TIP

Garam masala simply means hot spices and there is no fixed recipe. Most Indian cooks have their own favourite blend. While packets are available in the supermarkets, it's just as easy – and more satisfying – to make your own. It will keep for about 3 months in an airtight container. Dry-fry 5 dried red chillies, 1 cinnamon stick and 1 curry leaf in a heavy-based frying pan, stirring frequently, for about 1 minute. Stir in 1 tbsp each coriander and cumin seeds, ½ tsp each fenugreek seeds, black mustard seeds and black peppercorns and 6 cloves. Dry-fry over a very low heat, stirring or shaking the frying pan frequently, for 6–8 minutes. Remove from the heat and leave to cool, then grind to a powder in a spice grinder or with a pestle and mortar.

"I married the man who delivered the meat for my steak and chips... we've been married for 17 years — can't be bad!"

Rosemarie, Newbury

Steak & chips

9

There's no messing around with this dish — a particularly popular choice among the meat-eating male voters. All you have to decide is whether you want your steak rare or medium. This no-nonsense classic is ideal for those who just want to chill out at the end of the week.

SERVES 4

Preparation time: 15 minutes
Cooking time: 40–45 minutes

1 bunch of watercress

85 g/3 oz unsalted butter, softened

4 sirloin steaks, about 225 g/8 oz each

4 tsp Tabasco sauce

salt and pepper

OVEN CHIPS

450 g/1 lb potatoes, peeled

2 tbsp sunflower oil

VARIATION

If you like, substitute the same amount of fresh parsley for the watercress.

1 To make the chips, preheat the oven to 200°C/400°F/Gas Mark 6. Cut the potatoes into thick, even-sized chips. Rinse them under cold running water and then dry well on a clean tea towel. Place in a bowl, add the oil and toss together until coated.

2 Spread the chips on a baking sheet and cook in the preheated oven for 40–45 minutes, turning once, until golden.

3 Using a sharp knife, finely chop enough watercress to fill 4 tablespoons. Reserve a few watercress leaves for a garnish. Place the butter in a small bowl and beat in the chopped watercress with a fork until fully incorporated. Cover with clingfilm and leave to chill in the refrigerator until required.

4 Preheat the grill or barbecue. Sprinkle each steak with 1 teaspoon of the Tabasco sauce, rubbing it in well. Season to taste with salt and pepper.

5 Cook the steaks under the hot grill or over hot coals for 2½ minutes each side for rare, 4 minutes each side for medium and 6 minutes each side for well done. Transfer to serving plates, garnish with the reserved watercress leaves and serve immediately, topped with the watercress butter and accompanied by the chips.

COOK'S TIP

Sirloin is the most tender type of steak and may be sold as sirloin or under a variety of other names including entrecôte, porterhouse and T-bone, depending on which part of the loin has been cut and how. For a less expensive dish you could use rump steak, which is also a tender cut.

main courses

Lamb rogan josh
10

Reward yourself with this mouthwatering dish of tender lamb cooked in a colourful, creamy tomato sauce, and delicately flavoured with Indian spices. Lamb is India's favourite meat and this dish is truly something to linger over with love.

SERVES 4

Preparation time: 15 minutes
Cooling time: 5–10 minutes
Cooking time: 50–55 minutes

125 ml/4 fl oz ghee or
   vegetable oil

500 g/1 lb 2 oz boneless lamb,
   cut into bite-sized chunks

4 garlic cloves, chopped

3 fresh green chillies, deseeded
   and chopped

2.5-cm/1-inch piece fresh root
   ginger, grated

1 tsp poppy seeds

1 cinnamon stick, ground

1 cardamom pod, ground

4 cloves, ground

1 tsp coriander seeds, ground

1 tsp cumin seeds, ground

250 ml/9 fl oz soured cream

½ tsp ground turmeric

½ tsp chilli powder

2 large tomatoes, chopped

1 bay leaf

fresh coriander leaves, to
   garnish

freshly cooked rice, to serve

1 Heat half of the ghee in a large saucepan over a high heat, add the lamb and cook, stirring, for 5 minutes. Lift out the meat with a slotted spoon and drain on kitchen paper. Add the garlic, chillies, ginger, poppy seeds and ground spices to the saucepan and cook over a medium heat, stirring, for 4 minutes. Remove from the heat, cool for a few minutes, then transfer the spice mixture to a food processor. Stir in the soured cream, turmeric and chilli powder and process until smooth.

2 Heat the remaining ghee in the saucepan over a low heat, add the tomatoes and cook, stirring, for 3 minutes. Add the soured cream mixture and cook, stirring, until the oil separates. Remove from the heat and add the lamb. Add the bay leaf, return the saucepan to the heat and cover. Simmer gently for 35–40 minutes, or until most of the liquid has been absorbed. Remove from the heat and discard the bay leaf. Garnish with coriander leaves and serve with freshly cooked rice.

" Back to my place for a curry has become a Friday night ritual and, to be truthful, I love to show off my cooking. "

Toby, Leicester

desserts

Cheesecake

Chocoholics rule with this first-choice cheesecake. You have been good for the rest of the week so a wonderfully self-indulgent sweet on a Friday night is a well-deserved treat. It is so rich and creamy, you may even be able to leave a little to eat on Saturday.

SERVES 4–6

Preparation time: 20 minutes
Chilling time: 4 hours

BASE

4 tbsp butter, melted, plus
    extra for greasing

115 g/4 oz digestive biscuits,
    finely crushed

2 tsp unsweetened cocoa
    powder

halved kumquats, to decorate

CHOCOLATE LAYER

800 g/1 lb 12 oz mascarpone
    cheese

200 g/7 oz icing sugar, sifted

juice of ½ orange

finely grated rind of 1 orange

175 g/6 oz plain dark chocolate,
    melted

2 tbsp brandy

CHOCOLATE LEAVES

12–16 firm, fresh, smooth
    non-toxic leaves, such as bay
    or citrus

175 g/6 oz plain dark chocolate,
    broken into pieces

1 Grease a 20-cm/8-inch loose-bottomed cake tin.

2 To make the base, place the crushed biscuits, cocoa powder and melted butter in a large bowl and mix well. Press the biscuit mixture evenly over the base of the prepared tin.

3 Place the mascarpone and icing sugar in a bowl and stir in the orange juice and rind. Add the melted chocolate and brandy, and mix together until thoroughly combined. Spread the chocolate mixture evenly over the biscuit layer. Cover with clingfilm and chill for at least 4 hours.

4 To make the chocolate leaves, wipe the leaves gently with kitchen paper. Decide whether the upper or lower surfaces will produce the more interesting pattern. Heat a saucepan of water until it is barely simmering, then place the chocolate in a heatproof bowl and melt it by setting it over the saucepan of water, stirring occasionally. Remove from the heat and leave to cool slightly. Using a pastry brush or clean paintbrush, carefully coat one side of each leaf with the melted chocolate, working from the centre to the edges. Do not let the chocolate run over the edges or onto the other side of the leaves, as it will make them almost impossible to remove without breaking the decoration. Place the leaves, coated side up, on a sheet of baking paper to set. When the chocolate has set, carefully peel away the leaves from the stalk ends, handling the chocolate leaves as little as possible.

5 Remove the cheesecake from the refrigerator, turn out onto a serving platter and decorate with the chocolate leaves and kumquat halves. Serve immediately.

" I've never, ever had a bad cheesecake. All flavours, all variations are guaranteed to put me in a good mood! "

Ruth, Hadleigh

desserts

Ice cream

It's so luxurious, it's almost sinful. Home-made ice cream is just out of this world and with its rich texture and double chocolate flavours, this recipe is everything you could possibly want from a dessert. So set the mood for a wicked weekend.

SERVES 4

Preparation time: 30 minutes
Cooling time: 10 minutes
Cooking time: 5 minutes
Chilling time: 1½ hours
Freezing time: 2½ hours

6 egg yolks

100 g/3½ oz caster sugar

350 ml/12 fl oz milk

175 ml/6 fl oz double cream

100 g/3½ oz plain dark
  chocolate, chopped

75 g/2¾ oz white chocolate,
  grated or finely chopped

fresh mint leaves, to decorate

1 Place the egg yolks and sugar in a heatproof bowl and beat until fluffy. Heat the milk, cream and plain dark chocolate in a saucepan over a low heat, stirring, until melted and almost boiling. Remove from the heat and whisk into the egg mixture. Return the mixture to the pan and cook, stirring, over a low heat until thick. Do not let it simmer. Transfer to a heatproof bowl and cool. Cover with clingfilm and chill for 1½ hours. Remove from the refrigerator and stir in the white chocolate.

2 Transfer to a freezerproof container and freeze for 1 hour. Remove from the freezer, transfer to a bowl and whisk to break up the ice crystals. Return to the container and freeze for 30 minutes. Repeat twice more, freezing for 30 minutes and whisking each time. Alternatively, transfer the mixture to an ice cream machine and process for 15 minutes.

3 Scoop the ice cream into serving bowls, decorate with mint leaves and serve.

"It's not just better than sex, it's better than Sex and the City." *Fran, Wimbledon*

“We take turns choosing a Friday treat – and this is mine.”

Cathy, Wrexham

desserts

Fruit sorbet

Delicately flavoured and easy to make, this prettily coloured orange dessert has just the right amount of zing to round off an end-of-week supper, leaving you feeling satisfied and refreshed. It's a great choice for those with a sweet tooth but who are watching the calories.

SERVES 4

Preparation time: 25 minutes
Cooking time: 5 minutes
Cooling time: 15 minutes
Chilling time: 1 hour
Freezing time: 2½ hours

500 ml/18 fl oz water

200 g/7 oz caster sugar

4 large oranges

2 tbsp orange liqueur, such as Cointreau

4 scooped-out oranges, to serve

1 Heat the water and sugar in a saucepan over a low heat, stirring, until dissolved. Boil without stirring for 2 minutes. Pour into a heatproof bowl. Cool to room temperature. Grate the rind from 2 oranges and extract the juice. Extract the juice from 2 more oranges. Mix the juice and rind in a bowl, cover with clingfilm and reserve. Discard the squeezed oranges. Stir the orange juice, grated rind and orange liqueur into the cooled syrup. Cover with clingfilm and chill for 1 hour.

2 Transfer to a freezerproof container and freeze for 1 hour. Remove from the freezer, transfer to a bowl and whisk to break up the ice crystals. Return to the freezerproof container and freeze for 30 minutes. Repeat twice more, freezing for 30 minutes and whisking each time. Alternatively, transfer the mixture to an ice cream machine and process for 15 minutes.

3 Divide the frozen sorbet between the scooped-out orange cups and serve immediately.

COOK'S TIP
Citrus fruits, including oranges, are sometimes treated with an ethylene gas called diphenyl to keep their rinds bright and fresh looking. These are described as 'waxed'. If you cannot find untreated or 'unwaxed' oranges for grating, then scrub the rinds well under running water first.

desserts

Banana fritters 4

This is fun food both to cook and to eat and everybody – young, old and in-between – loves it. There is only one problem, which is that these bananas taste so unbelievably scrumptious that you may find yourself having to whisk up a second batch.

SERVES 4

Preparation time: 20 minutes
Cooking time: 10–12 minutes

70 g/2½ oz plain flour

2 tbsp rice flour

1 tbsp caster sugar

1 egg, separated

150 ml/5 fl oz coconut milk

4 large bananas

sunflower oil for deep-frying

TO DECORATE

1 tsp icing sugar

1 tsp ground cinnamon

lime wedges

COOK'S TIP

If you can buy the baby finger bananas that are popular for this dish in the East, leave them whole for coating and deep-frying.

1 Sift the plain flour, rice flour and sugar into a bowl and make a well in the centre. Add the egg yolk and coconut milk. Beat the mixture until a smooth, thick batter forms.

2 Whisk the egg white in a clean, dry bowl until stiff enough to hold soft peaks. Fold it into the batter lightly and evenly.

3 Heat a 6-cm/2½-inch depth of oil in a large saucepan to 180–190°C/350–375°F, or until a cube of bread browns in 30 seconds. Cut the bananas in half crossways, then dip them quickly into the batter to coat them.

4 Drop the bananas carefully into the hot oil and deep-fry in batches for 2–3 minutes until golden brown, turning once.

5 Drain on kitchen paper. Sprinkle with icing sugar and cinnamon and serve immediately, with lime wedges for squeezing juice as desired.

HOLIDAY ROMANCE

Top destination for light meals is stuffed tortillas, a Latin American speciality, while Spain scores the biggest vote with paella as the first choice for a main course. Tiramisù wins the vote not only in this category but also as the number one dessert of all.

light meals

Stuffed tortillas

A Mexican wave of opinion propels these tasty wraps to the top of the list. They're great as a snack or a light lunch, fabulous party food and the perfect solution when you have unexpected guests – not least because everybody can join in assembling them.

SERVES 4

Preparation time: 10–15 minutes
Cooling time: 10 minutes
Cooking time: 20–25 minutes

2 red peppers

4 good-quality pork or
  vegetarian sausages

325 g/11½ oz canned red
  kidney beans, drained, rinsed
  and drained again

4 large tomatoes, chopped

1 large onion, chopped

1 garlic clove, chopped

1 tbsp lime juice

1 tbsp chopped fresh basil

4 large wheat or corn tortillas,
  or 8 small ones

salt and pepper

TO SERVE

shredded lettuce

slices of fresh tomato

soured cream

1 Preheat the grill to medium. Place the red peppers on a baking sheet under the hot grill and cook for 10 minutes, turning frequently, until blackened and blistered all over. Using tongs, transfer to a polythene bag and leave for 10 minutes until cool enough to handle. Leave the grill switched on.

2 Cook the sausages under the grill, turning frequently, for 10–12 minutes until cooked right through. While the sausages are cooking, place the kidney beans, tomatoes, onion, garlic, lime juice and basil in a large bowl. Season to taste with salt and pepper and mix until well combined.

3 When the peppers are cool enough to handle, peel off their skins with your fingers. Halve and deseed, then cut the flesh into small pieces. Add the pepper to the kidney bean mixture. About 1 minute before the sausages are ready, warm the tortillas in a lightly greased, heavy-based or non-stick frying pan, or in a microwave, according to the packet instructions.

4 Remove the sausages from the grill and cut them into slices. Fill the tortillas with sausage slices, the kidney bean salsa, shredded lettuce, tomato slices and soured cream. Serve immediately.

" This makes me want to 'dance the night away with senoritas who can sway.' "

Alan, Cambridge

light meals

Tapas

A tapa, meaning a lid, was originally a slice of bread placed on top of a glass to prevent flies from getting into the sherry. Later, toppings were added and now tapas bars, with elaborate menus, have become fashionable in cities throughout Spain and the Western world.

Cracked marinated olives

SERVES 8 AS PART OF A TAPAS MEAL

Preparation time: 15 minutes
Marinating time: 8–15 days

450 g/1 lb can or jar unstoned
  large green olives, drained

4 garlic cloves, peeled but
  whole

2 tsp coriander seeds

1 small lemon

4 fresh thyme sprigs

4 feathery stalks of fennel

2 small fresh red chillies
  (optional)

pepper

Spanish extra virgin olive oil,
  to cover

1 To allow the flavours of the marinade to penetrate the olives, place on a chopping board and, using a rolling pin, bash them lightly so that they crack slightly. Alternatively, use a sharp knife to cut a lengthways slit in each olive as far as the stone.

2 Using the flat side of a broad knife, lightly crush each garlic clove. Using a pestle and mortar, crack the coriander seeds. Cut the lemon, with its rind, into small chunks.

3 Place the olives, garlic, coriander seeds, lemon chunks, thyme sprigs, fennel and chillies, if using, in a large bowl and toss together. Season

to taste with pepper (you should not need to add salt since conserved olives are usually salty enough). Pack the ingredients tightly into a glass jar with a lid. Pour in enough oil to cover the olives, then seal the jar tightly.

4 Leave the olives at room temperature for 24 hours, then marinate in the refrigerator for at least 1 week, preferably 2 weeks. Gently give the jar a shake occasionally to re-mix the ingredients. Return the olives to room temperature and remove from the oil to serve. Provide cocktail sticks for spearing the olives.

> " A glass of chilled wine, the sound of waves lapping on the beach and a fabulous selection of tapas — memories are made of this. "
>
> *Janice, Dundee*

Chorizo in red wine

SERVES 6 AS PART OF A TAPAS MEAL

Preparation time: 15 minutes
Marinating time: 8 hours
Cooking time: 20–25 minutes

200 g/7 oz chorizo sausage

200 ml/7 fl oz Spanish
  red wine

2 tbsp brandy *(optional)*

fresh flat-leaf parsley sprigs,
  to garnish

crusty bread, to serve

1 Before you begin, bear in mind that this dish is best if prepared the day before you are planning to serve it.

2 Using a fork, prick the chorizo sausage in 3 or 4 places. Place it in a large saucepan and pour in the wine. Bring the wine to the boil, then reduce the heat, cover and simmer gently for 15–20 minutes. Transfer the chorizo and wine to a bowl or dish, cover, and leave the sausage to marinate in the wine for 8 hours (best done overnight).

3 The next day, remove the chorizo from the bowl or dish and reserve the wine for later. Remove the outer casing from the chorizo and cut the sausage into 5-mm/¼-inch slices. Place the slices in a large, heavy-based frying pan or flameproof serving dish.

4 If you are adding the brandy, pour it into a small saucepan and heat gently. Then remove from the heat and pour over the chorizo slices, stand well back and set alight. When the flames have died down, shake the saucepan gently, add the reserved wine to the saucepan and cook over a high heat until almost all of the wine has evaporated.

5 Serve the chorizo in red wine piping hot, in the dish in which it was cooked, with parsley to garnish. Accompany with bread to mop up the juices and provide cocktail sticks to spear the pieces of chorizo.

light meals

Hummus

This Middle Eastern dip, made from chickpeas, garlic, lemon and tahini (a sesame seed paste) is a hugely popular starter, tastes great in sandwiches, features on loads of party buffet tables and, perhaps less famously, makes a wonderful accompaniment to grilled lamb chops.

SERVES 4

Soaking time: 8 hours
Preparation time: 10 minutes
Cooking time: 1 hour
Chilling time: 1 hour

115 g/4 oz dried chickpeas

3–6 tbsp lemon juice

3–6 tbsp water

2–3 garlic cloves, crushed

140 g/5 oz tahini

salt

TO GARNISH

1 tbsp olive oil

1 tsp cayenne pepper or
   paprika

1 fresh flat-leaf parsley sprig

TO SERVE

pitta bread *(see page 190)*

fresh green salad leaves

slices of fresh tomato

1 Soak the chickpeas overnight in enough cold water to cover them and allow room for expansion. Drain the chickpeas and boil in fresh water until tender – this will take about 1 hour. Drain.

2 To make the hummus, place the chickpeas in a food processor and blend with enough lemon juice and water to make a thick, smooth purée.

3 Add the garlic cloves. Mix well. Add the tahini and salt to taste.

Add more lemon juice or water if necessary to get the flavour and consistency that you want.

4 Spoon into a serving dish, drizzle over the oil and sprinkle with either cayenne pepper or paprika.

5 Cover with clingfilm and chill for at least 1 hour before serving. Garnish with a fresh parsley sprig and serve with pitta bread, fresh salad leaves and slices of cucumber and tomato.

light meals

Guacamole 4

There are many different versions of this pale green Mexican dip but all are based on avocado and contain chilli in some form or another, whether the chopped fresh pod or as Tabasco sauce. It's always delicious and is great served with tortilla chips or raw vegetable sticks.

SERVES 4

Preparation time: 10 minutes

2 ripe avocados

1 tomato

juice of 1 lime

1 tbsp sweet onion,
  finely chopped

2 tbsp fresh coriander,
  finely chopped

1 tbsp fresh red or green chilli,
  deseeded and finely chopped
  (optional)

1 fresh flat-leaf parsley sprig,
  to garnish

1 Cut the avocados in half, discard the stones and scoop the pulp into a large bowl. Mash to make a coarse paste.

2 Cut the tomato in half and remove all the seeds. Dice the flesh and add to the avocados.

3 Stir in the lime juice to loosen the mixture slightly, then stir in the onion, coriander and chilli, if using. Spoon into an attractive bowl and serve immediately, garnished with a parsley sprig.

COOK'S TIP
Any dish made with avocados will quickly discolour on exposure to the air, so don't make the guacamole too far in advance. The lime juice helps to slow down the process and if you do have to leave it to stand – no longer than 1 hour – cover the top of the dish with clingfilm.

" Making Guacamole with avocados picked from the garden is a memory to treasure forever. "

Lesley, Salisbury

light meals

Taramasalata

Made from smoked fish roe, originally grey mullet but more often cod these days, this Greek speciality is a feature of mezze menus, a selection of tempting starters or snacks, rather like tapas dishes. Once you've tasted this authentic home-made version, you'll understand why it is so popular.

SERVES 4

Preparation time: 10 minutes
Soaking time: 5 minutes

55 g/2 oz white bread

milk, to soak

75 g/2¾ oz smoked cod's roe

1 garlic clove, crushed

pinch of cayenne pepper

3–6 tbsp lemon juice

2–4 tbsp oil

TO GARNISH

slice of lemon, quartered

1 fresh flat-leaf parsley sprig

1 Remove the crusts from the bread, place in a bowl full of milk and soak for about 5 minutes, or until soft. Squeeze dry, reserving the liquid.

2 Combine the cod's roe, bread, garlic and cayenne pepper in a food processor and blend until smooth. Slowly add the lemon juice and oil, tasting frequently. Add the milk that was used to soak the bread if the consistency is not quite smooth enough.

3 Transfer to a serving dish and garnish with a quartered lemon slice and a parsley sprig. If not using immediately, cover with clingfilm and chill until 30 minutes before serving.

ACCOMPANIMENTS

To make pitta bread, sift together 450 g/1 lb strong white bread flour and a pinch of salt into a bowl and stir in 1½ tsp easy-blend dried yeast. Make a well in the centre and pour in 1 tbsp olive oil and about 225 ml/8 fl oz water. Using your fingers, gradually incorporate the dry ingredients into the liquid, adding a little more water if necessary to make a soft dough. Turn out onto a lightly floured surface and knead well until smooth and elastic. Form the dough into a ball, place in a well oiled bowl, cover with oiled clingfilm and leave to rise in a warm place for 1 hour, or until doubled in bulk. Turn out the dough and knead again briefly, then divide into 12 pieces. Flatten each piece with the palm of your hand into a 10-cm/4-inch round, brush with oil and space well apart on trays. Cover and leave to rise for 20 minutes. Meanwhile, preheat the oven, with 2 baking sheets inside, to 240°C/475°F/Gas Mark 9 or hotter if possible. Transfer the breads, in batches, to the hot baking sheets and bake for 3 minutes, then reduce the oven temperature to 230°C/450°F/Gas Mark 8 and bake for a further 3 minutes, until puffed up. Reheat the oven and the baking sheets between batches.

light meals

Tzatziki 6

This mint- and garlic-flavoured combination of cucumber and yogurt is freshness itself and a perfect mezze dish that immediately evokes memories of Aegean islands, magical sunsets and the gentle splash of waves. The only other thing you need is a glass of ouzo.

SERVES 4

Preparation time: 10 minutes
Chilling time: 2 hours

500 ml/18 fl oz natural
  Greek-style yogurt, or other
  thick natural yogurt
4 garlic cloves, very finely
  chopped
2 cucumbers, peeled, deseeded
  and very finely diced
1 tbsp lemon flavoured or extra
  virgin olive oil
3 tbsp lemon juice
1 tbsp chopped fresh mint
  leaves
salt and pepper

TO GARNISH
pinch of paprika
lemon wedge
1 fresh mint sprig

TO SERVE
celery, cut into sticks
carrots, cut into sticks
pitta bread, cut into triangles
(see page 190)

1 Place the yogurt, garlic, cucumber, oil, lemon juice and mint in a serving bowl and stir together until well combined. Season to taste with salt and pepper, cover with clingfilm, and leave to chill for at least 2 hours, or until required.

2 When ready to use, garnish with a pinch of paprika. Place on a plate garnished with a lemon wedge and parsley sprig and serve with celery, carrots and pitta bread triangles for dipping.

COOK'S TIP
Cucumber is naturally a very watery vegetable. In fact, it consists of about 95 per cent water. If you have time, it's a good idea to draw out some of this water. Place the diced cucumber in a sieve, sprinkling the layers generously with sea salt and leave to drain for about 1 hour. Rinse well and pat dry with a clean tea towel. Then proceed with the recipe.

" Pretending I was Zorba, I knocked a dish of tzatziki into the lap of my future wife. Not romantic, but we still laugh about it. "
Jon, Muswell Hill

light meals

Falafel

The **national dish of Egypt, these spicy patties, usually made from chickpeas but also sometimes from broad beans, are popular throughout North Africa and the Middle East. If you have spent a holiday anywhere from Morocco to Israel, these will be evocative and scrumptious little reminders.**

SERVES 4

Soaking time: 8 hours
Preparation time: 25 minutes
Cooking time: 1¼ hours
Resting time: 1 hour

225 g/8 oz dried chickpeas

1 large onion, finely chopped

1 garlic clove, crushed

2 tbsp chopped fresh parsley

2 tsp ground cumin

2 tsp ground coriander

½ tsp baking powder

vegetable oil, for deep-frying

salt and cayenne pepper

SERVING SUGGESTIONS
Hummus *(see page 186)*
tomato wedges
pitta bread *(see page 190)*

1 Soak the chickpeas overnight in enough cold water to cover them and allow room for expansion. Drain the chickpeas and boil in fresh water until tender – this will take about 1 hour. Drain.

2 Place the chickpeas in a food processor and process to make a coarse paste. Add the onion, garlic, seasoning, parsley, spices and baking powder and process again to mix.

3 Leave the mixture to rest for 30 minutes, then divide into 8 equal pieces. Shape each piece into a ball between the palms of your hands and arrange on a plate. Leave to rest for a further 30 minutes.

4 Heat the oil for deep-frying in a wok or deep saucepan. Gently drop in the balls and cook until golden brown. Carefully remove from the oil and drain for a few minutes on a plate lined with kitchen paper.

5 Serve the falafel hot or at room temperature with Hummus, accompanied by tomato wedges or sandwiched into pitta bread.

ACCOMPANIMENTS
Sesame and aubergine dip is delicious with falafel. Preheat the grill to medium. Place a large aubergine on a baking sheet under the hot grill and cook, turning frequently, until the skin is blackened and blistered all over. Using tongs, transfer to a work surface and when it's cool enough to handle, cut it in half and scoop out the flesh into a bowl. Mash coarsely with a fork. Gradually beat in 4 tbsp olive oil, 4 tbsp lemon juice and 4 tbsp tahini. Stir in 2 finely chopped garlic cloves. Taste and add more olive oil, lemon juice or tahini as required. Cover with clingfilm and store in the refrigerator until required. Remove the dip about 30 minutes before serving to bring it to room temperature. Meanwhile, dry-fry 1 tsp sesame seeds in a heavy-based frying pan until fragrant, then sprinkle them over the dip.

" Great memories of Cyprus — far too hot to go to the beach or sit by the pool so we went to the local eatery for a few bottles of beer and some Falafel — the best I ever tasted! "

Katherine, Dublin

" Nothing better than a day on the beach, then meeting up with friends to cook paella on an open fire. A full stomach, a glass of Rioja, great company and sneaking away to watch the stars come out with the girl I loved...(sigh!) "

Andy, Brentwood

main courses

Paella

Spain is still our number one holiday destination and paella is understandably the top main course in this category. There are probably as many versions of this colourful, one-pot, rice-based dish as there are cooks in the country, but this is one of the best.

SERVES 4

Preparation time: 15 minutes
Cooking time: 30 minutes

3 tbsp olive oil

2 tbsp butter

2 garlic cloves, chopped

1 onion, chopped

2 large tomatoes, deseeded and
  diced

150 g/5½ oz arborio rice

85 g/3 oz frozen peas

1 red pepper, deseeded and
  chopped

2 tsp dried mixed herbs

1 tsp powdered saffron

425 ml/15 fl oz chicken stock

4 skinless, boneless chicken
  breasts

150 g/5½ oz lean chorizo
  sausage, skinned

200 g/7 oz cooked lobster meat

200 g/7 oz raw prawns, peeled
  and deveined

1 tbsp chopped fresh flat-leaf
  parsley

salt and pepper

TO GARNISH

pinch of cayenne pepper

strips of red pepper

1 Heat the oil and butter in a large frying pan over a medium heat. Add the garlic and onion and cook, stirring, for about 3 minutes until slightly softened.

2 Add the tomatoes, rice, peas, red pepper, mixed herbs and saffron and cook, stirring, for 2 minutes. Pour in the stock and bring to the boil. Reduce the heat to low and cook, stirring, for 10 minutes.

3 Chop the chicken into small pieces and add to the frying pan. Cook, stirring occasionally, for 5 minutes. Chop the chorizo, add to the frying pan and cook for 3 minutes. Chop the lobster meat and add to the pan, along with the prawns and parsley. Season to taste with salt and pepper and cook, stirring, for a further 2 minutes.

4 Remove from the heat, transfer to a large serving platter or individual serving plates, garnish with cayenne and strips of red pepper and serve.

main courses

Vegetable moussaka

The Brits have shepherdess pie, the Italians have vegetarian lasagne and the Greeks have vegetable moussaka — and don't we love them all? Topped with aubergines and sliced potatoes rather than mash or pasta and coated in a creamy sauce, this vegetarian bake really hits the spot.

SERVES 4

Standing time: 30 minutes
Preparation time: 30 minutes
Cooking time: 1 hour 5 minutes

2 aubergines, about
  250 g/9 oz each, peeled and
  cut into chunks
5 tbsp olive oil, plus extra for
  oiling
2 garlic cloves, chopped
1 large onion, chopped
1 red pepper, deseeded and
  chopped
1 green pepper, deseeded and
  chopped
400 g/14 oz canned chopped
  tomatoes
1 courgette, sliced
1 tbsp chopped fresh rosemary
300 g/10½ oz waxy potatoes,
  such as Maris Peer, sliced
125 ml/4 fl oz single cream
175 g/6 oz ricotta cheese
2 eggs, beaten
salt and pepper
fresh crusty bread, to serve

1 Sprinkle the aubergine chunks with salt, then leave to stand for 30 minutes.

2 Heat the oil in a large saucepan over a medium heat. Add the garlic and onion and cook, stirring, for 3 minutes. Add the red and green peppers and cook for 5 minutes. Rinse the aubergine, drain, then add to the saucepan. Reduce the heat and cook, stirring, for 10 minutes.

3 Preheat the oven to 200°C/400°F/Gas Mark 6. Stir the tomatoes, courgette and rosemary into the aubergines. Season to taste, bring to the boil, then reduce the heat, cover and simmer for 10 minutes. Meanwhile, bring a saucepan of lightly salted water to the boil, add the sliced potatoes and cook for 5 minutes. Drain.

4 Mix the cream, ricotta and eggs in a bowl. Oil an ovenproof dish and spoon in the aubergine mixture. Top with the potatoes. Pour over the ricotta sauce. Bake for 30 minutes. Remove from the oven and divide between individual serving plates. Garnish with cayenne and rosemary sprigs. Serve with crusty bread.

" A plate of moussaka and a glass of retsina and I have to go and watch Shirley Valentine again. "

Debbie, Canterbury

TO GARNISH

pinch of cayenne pepper
fresh rosemary sprigs

main courses

Calzone

A cross between a pasty and an inside-out pizza, calzone was originally a snack to be eaten with the fingers, but has now become a tasty main course. Here, chargrilled Mediterranean vegetables acquire a wonderful sweetness and succulence that contrast superbly with the surrounding crust.

SERVES 4

Preparation time: 30 minutes
Rising and resting time: 1¼ hours
Cooking time: 35–45 minutes

DOUGH

225 g/8 oz plain white flour

1 tsp salt

½ tsp sugar

1 tsp easy-blend dried yeast

140 ml/4½ fl oz hand-hot water

2 tbsp olive oil, plus extra for oiling and brushing

FILLING

1 red onion, cut into wedges

2 garlic cloves, skin left on

2 baby aubergines, quartered lengthways

2 courgettes, halved lengthways

1 small red pepper, deseeded and quartered lengthways

1 small orange pepper, deseeded and quartered lengthways

4 tbsp olive oil

1 tbsp balsamic vinegar

1 tbsp chopped flat-leaf parsley

85 g/3 oz goat's cheese, diced

salt and pepper

1 Sift together the flour and salt into a bowl and stir in the sugar and yeast. Make a well in the centre and pour in the water and oil. Using your fingers, gradually incorporate the dry ingredients into the liquid. Put the dough into a clean bowl, cover with oiled clingfilm and leave to rise in a warm place for 1 hour, or until doubled in bulk.

2 Preheat the oven to 200°C/400°F/Gas Mark 6. Turn out the dough onto a lightly floured surface and knock back by punching with your fist. Knead briefly, then divide in half. Roll out each piece into a round about 5 mm/¼ inch thick and place on a baking sheet. Cover with lightly oiled clingfilm and leave to rest for 15 minutes.

3 Meanwhile, place the vegetables in a roasting tin. Combine the oil, vinegar, parsley and seasoning and pour over the top. Roast in the preheated oven for 15 minutes, turning once. Cool. Peel off the garlic and pepper skins and cover half of each dough round with vegetables and the goat's cheese, leaving a border. Brush the edges with water and fold the halves over and seal. Increase the oven temperature to 220°C/425°F/Gas Mark 7. Brush the dough with olive oil and bake for 20–30 minutes until golden.

> " We tried it with every filling possible and never had the same one twice! You can't beat hot calzone, a glass of wine and a good movie. "

Becster, Northampton

main courses

Risotto alla milanese

4

Saffron, the most expensive spice in the world, is the secret of the delicate flavour and beautiful golden colour of this classic Italian dish. Although it forms the traditional accompaniment to veal stew — osso bucco — it is frequently served on its own and is absolutely delicious.

SERVES 4

Preparation time: 10 minutes
Cooking time: 35–40 minutes

600 ml/1 pint chicken stock

125 g/4½ oz butter

900 g/2 lb skinless, boneless
  chicken breasts, thinly sliced

1 large onion, chopped

500 g/1 lb 2 oz risotto rice

150 ml/5 fl oz white wine

1 tsp crushed saffron threads

salt and pepper

fresh flat-leaf parsley sprigs,
  to garnish

55 g/2 oz freshly grated
  Parmesan cheese, to serve

1 Pour the stock into a saucepan and bring to the boil. Reduce the heat to a simmer.

2 Meanwhile, melt 55 g/2 oz of the butter in a deep frying pan. Add the chicken and onion and cook over a medium heat, stirring occasionally, for 8–10 minutes until golden brown.

3 Reduce the heat, add the rice and cook, stirring constantly, for a few minutes until the grains begin to swell and are thoroughly coated in the butter.

4 Add the wine and saffron and season to taste with salt and pepper. Cook, stirring constantly, until the wine has completely evaporated. Add 2 ladlefuls of the hot stock and cook, stirring constantly, until it has been completely absorbed. Add the remaining stock, 1 ladleful at a time, always stirring constantly. Allow each ladleful of stock to be absorbed before adding the next. When all the stock has been absorbed and the rice has a creamy texture, it is ready. This will take 20–25 minutes.

5 Garnish each individual plate with a parsley sprig, then serve the risotto immediately, sprinkled with the grated Parmesan cheese and dotted with the remaining butter.

" We spent our honeymoon in Italy and I fell in love all over again — this time with the country, the wine and the food. "

Claire, Warwick

main courses

Gnocchi romana

5

The gnocchi, or dumplings, are made from a mixture of semolina, milk and egg, which is allowed to set before being cut into rounds and baked with butter and grated Parmesan cheese. A filling dish, it's far tastier than it sounds, as visitors to the Eternal City will testify.

SERVES 4

Preparation time: 25 minutes
Cooling and chilling time:
 1½ hours
Cooking time: 40–45 minutes

700 ml/1¼ pints milk

pinch of freshly grated nutmeg

90 g/3¼ oz butter, plus extra for
 greasing

250 g/9 oz semolina

125 g/4½ oz freshly grated
 Parmesan cheese

2 eggs, beaten

vegetable oil, for oiling (optional)

55 g/2 oz Gruyère cheese,
 grated

salt and pepper

fresh basil sprigs, to garnish

1 Pour the milk into a saucepan and bring to the boil. Remove the saucepan from the heat and stir in the nutmeg, 25 g/1 oz of the butter and salt and pepper to taste.

2 Gradually stir the semolina into the milk, whisking to prevent lumps forming, and return the pan to a low heat. Simmer, stirring constantly, for 10 minutes until very thick.

3 Beat 60 g/2¼ oz of the Parmesan cheese into the semolina mixture, then beat in the eggs. Continue beating the mixture until smooth. Set the mixture aside for a few minutes to cool slightly.

4 Spread out the semolina mixture in an even layer on a sheet of baking paper or in a large, oiled baking tin, smoothing the surface with a damp spatula – it should be about 1 cm/½ inch thick.

Leave to cool completely, then leave to chill in the refrigerator for 1 hour.

5 Once chilled, cut out rounds of gnocchi, measuring about 4 cm/1½ inches in diameter, using a plain, greased pastry cutter.

6 Preheat the oven to 200°C/400°F/Gas Mark 6. Grease a shallow ovenproof dish. Lay the gnocchi trimmings in the base of the dish and cover with overlapping rounds of gnocchi.

7 Melt the remaining butter and drizzle over the gnocchi. Sprinkle over the remaining Parmesan cheese, then sprinkle over the Gruyère cheese.

8 Bake in the preheated oven for 25–30 minutes, or until the top is crisp and golden brown. Serve hot, garnished with the basil sprigs.

" I married my wife because she is so beautiful not, contrary to popular belief, because my mother-in-law makes the best gnocchi in Rome. "

Jason, Putney

" mmmm... Tiramisù does it every time for me... just delicious. "

Melanie, Merthyr Tydfil

desserts

Tiramisù

Literally meaning 'pick me up', this melt-in-the-mouth dessert has a reputation for doing exactly that, as its overwhelming vote proves. It's not a traditional dish, but since its invention about thirty years ago it has featured on favourite menus across the globe.

SERVES 4

Preparation time: 20 minutes
Chilling time: 2 hours

200 ml/7 fl oz strong black coffee, cooled to room temperature

4 tbsp orange liqueur, such as Cointreau

3 tbsp orange juice

16 Italian sponge fingers

250 g/9 oz mascarpone cheese

300 ml/10 fl oz double cream, lightly whipped

3 tbsp icing sugar

grated rind of 1 orange

60 g/2¼ oz chocolate, grated

TO DECORATE

chopped toasted almonds
crystallized orange peel
chocolate shavings

1 Pour the cooled coffee into a jug and stir in the orange liqueur and orange juice. Put 8 of the sponge fingers in the bottom of a serving dish, then pour over half of the coffee mixture.

2 Place the mascarpone in a separate bowl along with the cream, icing sugar and orange rind and mix together well. Spread half of the mascarpone mixture over the coffee-soaked sponge fingers, then arrange the remaining sponge fingers on top. Pour over the remaining coffee mixture and then spread over the remaining mascarpone mixture. Scatter over the grated chocolate and chill in the refrigerator for at least 2 hours. Serve decorated with chopped toasted almonds, crystallized orange peel and chocolate shavings.

desserts

Crème caramel

This creamy dessert with its caramelized topping is a favourite throughout Europe — called crème caramel in France, flan in Spain and, more mundanely, baked custard in Britain. The contrasting textures and flavours make it a top choice for adults and kids alike.

SERVES 4–6

Preparation time: 15 minutes
Cooking time: 1½–1¾ hours
Cooling and chilling time: 25 hours

butter, for greasing
175 g/6 oz plus 2 tbsp caster
  sugar
4 tbsp water
½ lemon
500 ml/18 fl oz milk
1 vanilla pod
2 large eggs
2 large egg yolks

TO DECORATE
sugared fruit
fresh mint leaves

1 Preheat the oven to 160°C/325°F/Gas Mark 3. Lightly grease the side of a 1.2-litre/2-pint soufflé dish. To make the caramel, place 75 g/2¾ oz sugar with the water in a saucepan over a medium–high heat and cook, stirring, until the sugar dissolves. Boil until the syrup turns a deep golden brown.

2 Immediately remove from the heat and add in a few drops of lemon juice. Pour into the soufflé dish and swirl around. Reserve.

3 Pour the milk into a saucepan. Slit the vanilla pod lengthways and add it to the milk. Bring to the boil, remove the saucepan from the heat and stir in the remaining sugar, stirring until it dissolves. Reserve.

4 Beat the eggs and egg yolks together in a bowl. Pour the milk mixture over them, whisking. Remove the vanilla pod. Strain the egg mixture into a bowl, then transfer to the soufflé dish.

5 Place the dish in a roasting tin with enough boiling water to come two-thirds up the side.

6 Bake in the preheated oven for 75–90 minutes, or until a knife inserted in the centre comes out clean. Leave to cool completely. Cover with clingfilm and leave to chill for at least 24 hours.

7 Run a round-bladed knife around the edge. Place an up-turned serving plate with a rim on top, then invert the plate and dish, giving a sharp shake halfway over. Lift off the soufflé dish and serve, decorated with sugared fruit and fresh mint leaves.

" Holiday in Greece last year, sitting in a restaurant on the sea front watching the sun set. Mmmmm... "

Emma, Colchester

desserts

Baklava

Versions of this sticky pastry are made throughout the Mediterranean and Middle East but perhaps the best known is the honey-soaked Greek variety. All of them consist of flaky layers of crisp pastry with a sweetened filling of nuts, drenched in a syrupy coating.

SERVES 4

Preparation time: 30 minutes
Cooking time: 1 hour
Cooling time: 1 hour

150 g/5½ oz shelled pistachio
  nuts, finely chopped
75 g/2¾ oz toasted hazelnuts,
  finely chopped
75 g/2¾ oz blanched
  hazelnuts, finely chopped
grated rind of 1 lemon
1 tbsp brown sugar
1 tsp ground mixed spice
150 g/5½ oz butter, melted,
  plus extra for greasing
250 g/9 oz (about 16 sheets)
  frozen filo pastry, thawed
250 ml/9 fl oz water
2 tbsp clear honey
1 tbsp lemon juice
300 g/10½ oz caster sugar
½ tsp ground cinnamon

1 Preheat the oven to 160°C/325°F/Gas Mark 3. Place the nuts, lemon rind, sugar and mixed spice in a bowl and mix well. Grease a round cake tin, 18 cm/7 inches in diameter and 5 cm/2 inches deep, with butter. Cut the whole stack of filo sheets to the size of the tin. Keep the filo rounds covered with a damp tea towel. Lay 1 round on the base of the tin and brush with melted butter. Add another 6 rounds on top, brushing between each layer with melted butter. Spread over one-third of the nut mixture, then add 3 rounds of buttered filo. Spread over another third of nut mixture then top with 3 more rounds of buttered filo. Spread over the remaining nut mixture and add the last 3 rounds of buttered filo. Cut into wedges, then bake in the oven for 1 hour.

2 Meanwhile, place the water, honey, lemon juice, caster sugar and cinnamon in a saucepan. Bring to the boil, stirring. Reduce the heat and simmer, without stirring, for 15 minutes. Cool. Remove the baklava from the oven, pour over the syrup and leave to set before serving.

VARIATION
To make an orange-flavoured syrup, substitute 2 tsp finely grated orange rind for the lemon juice and use orange blossom honey instead of blended. This goes especially well with baklava made with almonds instead of pistachios.

COOK'S TIP
If you can bear to leave it that long, baklava can be stored for up to 1 week in an airtight container.

desserts

Zabaglione

This dessert is so light and frothy it seems almost to be a figment of the imagination, although it clearly registered among the holiday memories of the voters. The classic version is made with Marsala, a sweet wine from the island of Sicily, and it should always be served barely warm.

SERVES 4

Preparation time: 5 minutes
Cooking time: 10–15 minutes

4 egg yolks
70 g/2½ oz caster sugar
125 ml/4 fl oz Marsala wine
amaretti biscuits, to serve

1 Half-fill a saucepan with water and bring to the boil. Reduce the heat so that the water is barely simmering. Whisk the egg yolks and sugar in a bowl, preferably with an electric whisk, until pale and creamy.

2 Set the bowl over the saucepan of water. Do not let the base touch the surface of the water, or the egg yolks will scramble.

3 Gradually add the Marsala wine, whisking constantly. Continue whisking until the mixture is thick and has increased in volume. Pour into heatproof glasses or bowls and serve immediately with amaretti biscuits.

VARIATION
Decorate the zabaglione with slit strawberries, placed on the rim of each glass, or serve with sponge fingers or crisp biscuits.

COOK'S TIP
You can make zabaglione with a balloon whisk, but it may take as long as 20 minutes to cook. It is important that the mixture is not cooked for too long and does not get too hot, as this will make it separate. It will also separate if it is left to stand for more than a few minutes before serving.

❝ I eventually married the waiter who spent ten minutes teaching me to pronounce a dessert that's easier to eat than say. ❞

Sheila, Peterborough

NEW WAVE

Top of the list of light meals and the overall winning recipe is chicken satay. The most popular main course is fajitas, an equally fiery dish from Mexico. The almost – but only almost – unbearably sweet banoffee pie took the desserts medal.

light meals

Chicken satay

1

A great light meal, this would also be the perfect starter, if wasn't so tempting that taking 'just one more' is almost irresistible. These succulent, South-east Asian chicken kebabs, served with a piquant peanut sauce, are always popular at parties and barbecues too.

SERVES 8

Preparation time: 20 minutes
Marinating time: 1 hour
Cooking time: 10 minutes

900 g/2 lb skinless, boneless
  chicken breast meat, cut
  into 5-mm/¼-inch thick,
  2.5-cm/1-inch wide strips

MARINADE

2 tbsp vegetable oil

2 tbsp soy sauce

2 tsp tamarind paste

1 lemon-grass stalk
  (tender inner part only),
  roughly chopped

2 garlic cloves, crushed

1 tsp ground cumin

1 tsp ground coriander

1 tbsp lime juice

1 tsp soft light brown sugar

PEANUT SAUCE

2 tbsp smooth peanut butter

200 ml/7 fl oz coconut cream

2 tsp red Thai curry paste
  (see page 243)

1 tbsp Thai fish sauce

1 tbsp soft light brown sugar

1 Thread the chicken onto presoaked bamboo skewers.

2 To make the marinade, place the oil, soy sauce, tamarind paste, lemon grass, garlic, cumin, coriander, lime juice and sugar in a food processor and blend to make a paste. Transfer to a bowl.

3 Add the chicken to the marinade and toss to coat. Cover with clingfilm and chill for at least 1 hour to marinate.

4 To make the peanut sauce, place the peanut butter, coconut cream, curry paste, fish sauce and sugar in a saucepan. Heat gently, stirring, to form a smooth sauce. Remove from the heat and reserve.

5 Preheat the grill or barbecue. Cook the chicken under the hot grill or over hot coals for 3–5 minutes on each side, or until cooked through. Reheat the sauce, adding a little hot water if necessary, and serve with the chicken.

" Chicken satay always brings back good memories of a very romantic holiday in Malaysia with my husband... "

Sharon, London

COOK'S TIP

The specialist ingredients required are available from some large supermarkets, as well as Japanese and other Asian food shops. Kombu is a brownish-green seaweed that is part of the kelp family. It is often sold in dried sheets. Nori is also a kind of seaweed with a sweet flavour. It may be toasted before it is used or you can buy ready-toasted nori, called yaki-nori. Sushi rice has a round grain and becomes slightly sticky when cooked so that it can be moulded. Pickled ginger is pale pink and the traditional condiment served with sushi to refresh the palate in between mouthfuls. Wasabi, also a traditional accompaniment to sushi, is a very hot, green horseradish. It is sold as a paste or in powder form, which then has to be mixed with water rather like mustard powder.

light meals

Japanese sushi

Japanese food has enjoyed an unprecedented rise in popularity over the last decade, not only because of its distinctive flavours, but also because it looks so lovely. This sushi, with smoked salmon and cucumber, is a work of art that gives as much pleasure to creative cooks in its preparation as it does to discerning diners.

SERVES 4

Preparation time: 30 minutes
Cooking time: 15 minutes
Standing time: 15 minutes
Chilling time: 15 minutes

125 g/4½ oz sushi rice

165 ml/5½ fl oz water

1 piece of kombu (optional)

1 tbsp sushi rice seasoning

vegetable oil, for oiling

2 tbsp Japanese mayonnaise

200 g/7 oz smoked salmon

½ cucumber, peeled and cut
  into very thin slices

shredded nori, to garnish

TO SERVE

pickled ginger

wasabi paste

1 Wash the sushi rice under cold running water until the water running through it is completely clear, then drain. Place the rice in a saucepan with the water and the kombu (if you are using it), then cover and bring to the boil as quickly as you can. Remove the kombu, turn the heat down and simmer for 10 minutes. Turn off the heat and leave the rice to stand for 15 minutes. Do not at any point take the lid off the saucepan once you have removed the kombu.

2 Place the hot rice in a large, shallow bowl and pour the sushi rice seasoning evenly over the surface of the rice. Now you will need to use both hands, one to mix the seasoning into the rice with quick cutting strokes using a spatula and the other to fan the sushi rice in order to cool it down as quickly as you can. Mix the seasoning in carefully – you do not want to break a single rice grain. The sushi rice should look shiny and be at room temperature when ready.

3 Oil a terrine tin (preferably with drop-down sides) and line it with a piece of clingfilm so that the clingfilm hangs over the edges. (This helps to pull the sushi out afterwards.) Pack the tin 3 cm/1¼ inches full with the rice. Spread a layer of mayonnaise on top of the rice. Arrange the smoked salmon and cucumber in diagonal strips on top of the rice, doubling up the smoked salmon layers if you have enough so that the topping is nice and thick. Cover the top of the rice with a strip of clingfilm, place another terrine tin on top and add something heavy, such as a few cans of tomatoes, to weight it.

4 Chill the sushi for 15 minutes, take off the tin and weights and pull out the sushi. Cut the sushi into 8–10 pieces with a wet, sharp knife. Place on a serving plate garnished with shredded nori and serve with pickled ginger and wasabi paste.

Sushi is made using both raw and cooked fish. If you use raw fish this is at your own risk. Raw fish has more bacteria and parasites than cooked fish. Some diseases, such as diabetes and liver disease, preclude you from eating raw fish or shellfish. Please consult your doctor if in doubt. Mercury levels also tend to be higher in long-lived, larger fish with darker meat such as swordfish, king mackerel and tuna. Pregnant women, nursing mothers and young children should avoid eating these types of fish.

If you use raw fish, buy it from a good supplier or shop that sells 'sushi or sashimi grade' fish. Buy shellfish that comes from certified water and, once bought, chill it immediately and use on the same day. Prepare everything else before taking the fish out of the refrigerator, keeping everything very clean, and serve immediately.

light meals

Moroccan couscous salad

Couscous is a traditional ingredient throughout North Africa but the grains require considerable skill and time to prepare properly. The invention of ready-prepared couscous overcame this problem and resulted in instant popularity across Europe.

SERVES 4

Preparation time: 20 minutes
Cooking time: 15–20 minutes
Cooling time: 45 minutes

225 g/8 oz couscous

1 cinnamon stick, about
  5 cm/2 inches long

2 tsp coriander seeds

1 tsp cumin seeds

2 tbsp olive oil

1 small onion, finely chopped

2 garlic cloves, finely chopped

½ tsp ground turmeric

pinch of cayenne pepper

1 tbsp lemon juice

50 g/1¾ oz sultanas

3 ripe plum tomatoes, chopped

85 g/3 oz cucumber, chopped

4 spring onions, sliced

200 g/7 oz canned tuna in olive
  oil, drained and flaked

3 tbsp chopped fresh coriander

salt and pepper

1 Prepare the couscous according to the packet instructions, omitting any butter if recommended. Transfer to a large bowl and reserve until required.

2 Heat a small frying pan and add the cinnamon stick, coriander seeds and cumin seeds. Dry-fry over a high heat until the seeds begin to pop and smell fragrant. Remove from the heat and pour the seeds and cinnamon into a mortar. Grind with a pestle to a fine powder. Alternatively, grind in a spice grinder. Reserve.

3 Heat the oil in a clean frying pan and add the onion. Cook over a low heat for 7–8 minutes until softened and lightly browned. Add the garlic and cook for a further 1 minute. Stir in the roasted and ground spices, turmeric and cayenne and cook for a further 1 minute. Remove from the heat and stir in the lemon juice. Add this mixture to the couscous and mix together well, ensuring that all of the grains are coated.

4 Add the sultanas, tomatoes, cucumber, spring onions, tuna and chopped coriander. Season to taste with salt and pepper and mix together. Leave to cool before serving at room temperature.

VARIATION

Moroccan grain salads often feature a mixture of rice and couscous. Cook 175 g/6 oz long grain rice in a large pan of lightly salted, boiling water for about 15 minutes until tender. Drain well, transfer it to the bowl with the couscous and mix, fluffing up the grains with a fork.

"It's taken a while for Mexican food to come to Britain, but now it's here, it's here big time." *Ken, York*

light meals

Cheese & bean quesadillas

Tortillas filled with a typically flavoursome Mexican mixture of cheese, beans, onion and salsa make enticing snacks and, served with salad, a filling light lunch. Here, they are heated to melt the cheese but, if you like, you can fry them in corn oil until golden brown on both sides.

SERVES 4–6

Preparation time: 20 minutes
Cooking time: 10 minutes

corn oil, for brushing

8 flour tortillas

200 g/7 oz canned black haricot beans, drained, or refried beans

200 g/7 oz Cheddar cheese, grated

1 onion, chopped

½ bunch of fresh coriander leaves, chopped, plus extra to garnish

1 quantity salsa (see page 227)

1 Lightly brush a heavy-based or non-stick frying pan with the oil and gently warm the tortillas. (Alternatively, warm them in the microwave, according to the packet instructions.)

2 Remove the tortillas from the frying pan and quickly spread with a layer of warm beans. Top each tortilla with grated cheese, onion, fresh coriander and a spoonful of salsa. Roll up tightly.

3 Just before serving, heat the non-stick frying pan over a medium heat, sprinkling lightly with a drop or two of water. Add the tortilla rolls, cover the pan and heat through until the cheese melts. Leave to lightly brown, if wished.

4 Remove from the frying pan and slice each roll, on the diagonal, into about 4 bite-sized pieces. Serve the dish immediately.

COOK'S TIP

To prepare refried beans, soak 350 g/12 oz dried black haricot or red kidney beans in cold water for 4 hours, then drain and place in a saucepan. Add 1 chopped onion, 1 chopped garlic clove, 2 deseeded and chopped fresh green chillies and sufficient cold water to cover. Bring to the boil and boil vigorously for 15 minutes, then reduce the heat and simmer for 30 minutes. Add 1 tbsp corn oil and simmer for a further 30 minutes. Season with salt and cook for a further 30 minutes until tender. Meanwhile, heat 1 tbsp corn oil in a frying pan and cook 1 chopped onion and 1 chopped garlic clove over a low heat, stirring occasionally, for 5 minutes, until softened. Stir in 2 peeled and deseeded, chopped tomatoes and cook for 3 minutes more. Remove the beans from the heat and transfer 3 tbsp to the frying pan. Cook, mashing them to a paste. Return the pan of beans to a low heat, add the mashed bean mixture and cook, stirring gently, until the liquid has thickened. To refry the beans, melt 85 g/3 oz lard in a frying pan. Add 1 chopped onion and cook over a low heat, stirring occasionally, for 5 minutes, until softened. Add about one-third of the cooked beans to the pan and cook, mashing them well with a wooden spoon. Add the remaining beans in 2 batches, together with another 25 g/1 oz lard. Cook and mash until the beans have formed a coarse, thick paste.

Jamaican rice & peas

In Jamaica it's called rice and peas, in Barbados it's called peas and rice — but peas don't feature in any of the Caribbean islands' recipes. However, this healthy combination of grain and pulses — a perfect protein partnership — is a tasty and filling lunch dish.

SERVES 6–8

Soaking time: 8 hours
Preparation time: 20 minutes
Cooking time: 1½–2¾ hours
Standing time: 5 minutes

450 g/1 lb dried beans, such as black-eyed beans, black beans or small red kidney beans, soaked in cold water overnight

2 tbsp vegetable oil

1 large onion, chopped

2–3 garlic cloves, finely chopped

2 fresh red chillies, deseeded and chopped

450 g/1 lb long-grain white rice

400 ml/14 fl oz canned coconut milk

¾ tsp dried thyme

salt

TOMATO SALSA

4 ripe tomatoes, deseeded and cut into 5-mm/¼-inch pieces

1 red onion, finely chopped

4 tbsp chopped fresh coriander

2 garlic cloves, finely chopped

1–2 fresh jalapeño chillies, deseeded and thinly sliced

1–2 tbsp extra virgin olive oil

1 tbsp fresh lime juice

1 tsp light brown sugar

salt and pepper

TO GARNISH

slices of lime

fresh coriander leaves

fresh bird's eye chillies

1 Drain the soaked beans, rinse and place in a large saucepan. Cover generously with cold water and bring to the boil over a high heat, skimming off any foam.

2 Boil the beans for about 10 minutes (to remove any toxins), drain and rinse and drain again. Return to the saucepan, cover with cold water again and bring to the boil over a high heat.

3 Reduce the heat and keep at a medium simmer, partially covered, for about 1¼–1½ hours for black-eyed beans, 1½–2 hours for black beans or 50–60 minutes for kidney beans until tender. Drain, reserving the cooking liquid.

4 Heat the oil in another saucepan. Add the onion and cook for about 2 minutes until softened. Stir in the garlic and chillies and cook for a further 1 minute. Add the rice and stir until well coated.

5 Stir in the coconut milk, thyme and about 1 teaspoon salt. Add the cooked beans and 450 ml/16 fl oz of the reserved bean cooking liquid to cover; add more bean liquid if necessary. Bring the mixture to the boil, then reduce the heat to low, cover tightly and cook for 20–25 minutes.

6 Meanwhile, make the tomato salsa: combine all the ingredients in a bowl and stand, loosely covered, at room temperature.

7 Remove the rice from the heat and stand, covered, for 5 minutes, then fork into a serving bowl. Serve hot with the salsa on individual plates garnished with lime slices, fresh coriander leaves and bird's eye chillies.

main courses

Classic fajitas

These hot-shot wraps from Mexico have certainly taken Britain — and the voters — by storm. Traditionally the steak is served, still sizzling, in the pan in which it was cooked and it certainly looks and sounds impressive when it's placed on the table.

SERVES 4

Preparation time: 25 minutes
Marinating time:
 30 minutes–8 hours
Cooking time: 15 minutes

**700 g/1 lb 9 oz beef skirt steak
 or tender steak, cut into strips**

6 garlic cloves, chopped

juice of 1 lime

large pinch of mild chilli powder

large pinch of paprika

large pinch of ground cumin

1–2 tbsp extra virgin olive oil

salt and pepper

corn oil, for brushing

12 flour tortillas

vegetable oil, for frying

**1–2 avocados, stoned, sliced
 and tossed with lime juice**

125 ml/4 fl oz soured cream

PICO DE GALLO SALSA

8 ripe tomatoes, diced

3 spring onions, sliced

**1–2 fresh green chillies,
 deseeded and chopped**

3–4 tbsp chopped fresh coriander

5–8 radishes, diced

ground cumin

1 Combine the beef with half the garlic, half the lime juice, the chilli powder, paprika, cumin and olive oil. Add salt and pepper, mix well and leave to marinate for at least 30 minutes at room temperature, or overnight in the refrigerator.

2 To make the salsa, place the tomatoes in a small bowl with the spring onions, green chillies, coriander and radishes. Season to taste with cumin, salt and pepper. Reserve until required.

3 Lightly brush a heavy-based or non-stick frying pan with the corn oil and gently warm the tortillas. Wrap in foil as you work, to keep them warm.

4 Heat a little vegetable oil in another frying pan over a high heat and stir-fry the meat until browned and just cooked through.

5 Serve the sizzling hot meat with the warm tortillas, the salsa, avocado and soured cream for each person to make his or her own rolled-up fajitas.

"I love experimenting with new recipes, especially as my kid's food diary and Mexican pronunciation are a nightmare for her teacher." *Sarah, Sidcup*

main courses

Chicken cajun-style

2

Spices, especially cayenne pepper, are the hallmarks of Cajun cuisine, an unlikely blend of French peasant cooking and local ingredients from the swamplands of Louisiana. Already massively popular throughout the United States, it's now becoming very fashionable in Britain.

SERVES 4

Preparation time: 15 minutes
Marinating time: 1 hour
Cooking time: 15 minutes

16 chicken wings

4 tsp paprika

2 tsp ground coriander

1 tsp celery salt

1 tsp ground cumin

½ tsp cayenne pepper

½ tsp salt

1 tbsp vegetable oil

2 tbsp red wine vinegar

fresh parsley sprigs, to garnish

TO SERVE

cherry tomatoes

mixed salad leaves

**sauce, such as chilli salsa or
  soured cream and chive dip**

COOK'S TIP
To save time, you can buy ready-made Cajun spice seasoning to rub over the chicken wings.

1 Remove the wing tips of the chicken with kitchen scissors.
2 Mix the paprika, ground coriander, celery salt, ground cumin, cayenne pepper, salt, oil and vinegar together in a bowl.
3 Rub this mixture over the wings to coat evenly and leave to marinate in the refrigerator for at least 1 hour to allow the flavours to permeate the chicken.

4 Preheat the grill or barbecue. Cook the chicken wings under the hot grill or over hot coals, occasionally brushing with oil and turning frequently for 15 minutes, or until cooked through.
5 Garnish the chicken with parsley sprigs and serve with cherry tomatoes, mixed salad leaves and a sauce of your choice.

" Cajun chicken – so simple, yet tastes great. "

Victoria, Inverness

"Tried Thai green curry in UK — it was good — so I had to go to Thailand to try the real thing — superb!" *Debra, Paignton*

main courses

Thai green curry

Thai cooking in general and Thai curries in particular have rocketed up our list of favourite foods in the last decade or so. The quality of some so-called Thai restaurants may be dubious, but this classic is easily made at home, takes very little time and tastes superb.

SERVES 4

Preparation time: 10 minutes
Cooking time: 20 minutes

150 g/5½ oz broccoli florets

150 g/5½ oz mangetout

2 tbsp chilli oil

2 tbsp Thai green curry paste

350 ml/12 fl oz coconut milk

200 g/7 oz firm marinated tofu,
  cut into cubes

1 green pepper, deseeded and
  sliced

1 yellow pepper, deseeded and
  sliced

1 tbsp soy sauce

100 g/3½ oz beansprouts

1 tbsp chopped fresh coriander

salt and pepper

fresh coriander sprigs,
  to garnish

freshly cooked noodles, to serve

1 Bring a large saucepan of water to the boil, add the broccoli and mangetout and cook for 2 minutes. Drain, refresh under cold running water, then drain again.

2 Heat the oil in a large saucepan over a medium heat, add the curry paste and cook, stirring, for 1 minute. Stir in 4 tablespoons of the coconut milk, then add the tofu, broccoli, mangetout, peppers and soy sauce. Cook for 5 minutes, then stir in the remaining coconut milk and bring to the boil. Reduce the heat, add the beansprouts and cook for a further 5 minutes. Stir in the chopped coriander, season to taste with salt and pepper and heat through.

3 Remove from the heat and spoon onto freshly cooked noodles. Garnish with coriander sprigs and serve.

Mushroom risotto

All the classic risotto recipes come from northern Italy because that's where the essential ingredients — round-grain risotto rice, butter and Parmesan cheese — are produced. When you taste this creamy dish, it's easy to see why it used to be illegal to export the much-prized special rice.

SERVES 4

Preparation time: 10 minutes
Cooking time: 35–45 minutes

850 ml/1½ pints vegetable
  stock

3 tbsp olive oil

2 large garlic cloves, crushed

400 g/14 oz mushrooms, sliced

40 g/1½ oz butter

4 shallots, chopped

250 g/9 oz risotto rice

2 tbsp white wine

1 tbsp lemon juice

finely grated rind of ½ lemon

1 tbsp chopped fresh parsley

1 tbsp chopped fresh coriander

salt and pepper

fresh coriander sprigs, to
  garnish

1 Pour the stock into a saucepan and bring to the boil. Reduce the heat to a simmer. Meanwhile, heat the oil in a large frying pan over a low heat, add the garlic and mushrooms and cook, stirring, for 3 minutes. Remove from the heat and reserve.

2 Heat the butter in a large saucepan over a medium heat, add the shallots and cook, stirring, for 3 minutes. Add the rice and cook, stirring constantly, for 2 minutes, then pour in the wine and lemon juice and stir until the liquid is almost absorbed. Add a ladleful of the simmering stock, and cook, stirring, until it is absorbed. Keep adding the stock, a ladleful at a time and stirring constantly, waiting for each ladleful to be absorbed before adding the next.

3 When all the liquid has almost been absorbed, stir in the mushrooms, lemon rind and salt and pepper to taste. Continue to cook, stirring, until the liquid has been completely absorbed, then remove from the heat and stir in the parsley and coriander. Serve immediately, garnished with coriander sprigs.

main courses

Jerk chicken

This Jamaican speciality is guaranteed to turn any barbecue into a carnival, although it can, of course, be cooked under the grill too. Jerk spices were originally used for cooking pork, but this chicken version certainly scores highly in this rather colder island.

SERVES 4

Preparation time: 15 minutes
Marinating time: 24 hours
Cooking time: 30 minutes

4 chicken portions
1 bunch of spring onions,
  trimmed
1–2 fresh Scotch bonnet
  chillies, deseeded
1 garlic clove
5-cm/2-inch piece fresh root
  ginger, roughly chopped
½ tsp dried thyme
½ tsp paprika
¼ tsp ground allspice
pinch of ground cinnamon
pinch of ground cloves
4 tbsp white wine vinegar
3 tbsp light soy sauce
pepper

COOK'S TIP
As Jamaican cuisine becomes increasingly popular, you will find jars of ready-made jerk marinade, which you can use when time is short. Allow the chicken to marinate for as long as possible for maximum flavour.

1 Rinse the chicken portions and pat them dry on kitchen paper. Place them in a shallow dish.

2 Place the spring onions, chillies, garlic, ginger, thyme, paprika, allspice, cinnamon, cloves, wine vinegar, soy sauce and pepper to taste in a food processor and process to make a smooth mixture.

3 Pour the spicy mixture over the chicken. Turn the chicken portions over so that they are well coated in the marinade. Transfer the chicken to the refrigerator and leave to marinate for up to 24 hours.

4 Preheat the grill or barbecue. Remove the chicken from the marinade and cook under the hot grill or over hot coals for about 30 minutes, turning the chicken over and basting occasionally with any remaining marinade, until the chicken is cooked through.

5 Transfer the chicken portions to individual serving plates and serve immediately.

COOK'S TIP
Scotch bonnet chillies are fiery hot. They are related to, although not the same as, habanero chillies, the hottest variety known. They are the exception that proves the rule that small pointed chillies are usually much hotter than short, blunt ones as they acquired their name because their rounded shape is reminiscent of a floppy hat. The heat of chillies, which derives from a volatile oil called capsaicin, is not in fact in the seeds but in the membranes surrounding them. Deseeding the pods also removes the membranes.

main courses

Thai fish cakes

Usually served as a starter in Thailand, these crisp, spicy morsels have become so popular that they are eaten here as a main course. To restore a level of cultural authenticity, you could serve them with a glass of Thai beer, such as Amarit or Singha.

SERVES 4

Preparation time: 15 minutes
Chilling time: 30 minutes
Cooking time: 20–30 minutes

500 g/1 lb 2 oz skinless,
  boneless cod fillet, cut
  into chunks
1 tbsp Thai red curry paste
  (see page 243)
1 egg, beaten
1 tsp light muscovado sugar
1 tsp salt
1 tbsp cornflour
75 g/2¾ oz green beans,
  finely chopped
1 tbsp chopped fresh coriander
4 tbsp vegetable oil, for frying
lime wedges, to garnish

SERVING SUGGESTIONS
salad
stir-fried green vegetables,
  such as beans, broccoli
  or mangetout

1 Place the cod into in a food processor and chop roughly. Add the curry paste, egg, sugar, salt and cornflour. Blend well.

2 Stir in the green beans and chopped coriander.

3 Transfer to a bowl, cover with clingfilm and chill in the refrigerator for 30 minutes. Roll the mixture into 12 balls, then flatten each ball into a 5-cm/2-inch cake.

4 Heat the oil in a frying pan over a medium heat and cook the cakes in batches for about 3 minutes on each side, or until golden brown and cooked through. Keep the cooked fish cakes warm while frying the remainder.

5 Garnish with the lime wedges and serve with salad or stir-fried green vegetables such as beans, broccoli or mangetout.

COOK'S TIP
Cod is fast becoming an endangered species, so make sure that you are buying fish caught from a sustainable source. Alternatively, substitute another white fish, such as haddock or one of the increasingly common imports from the southern hemisphere.

"My Mum makes fabulous English fish cakes but even she was impressed when I served up their Thai cousins. So, secretly, was I."

Joanna, Northampton

main courses

Lamb couscous 7

North African food is a relatively recent – and rather joyous – discovery in this country for most people. Fragrant, Moroccan tagines with their combination of meat and dried fruit, served with couscous, have become popular both as family meals and for entertaining.

SERVES 4

Preparation time: 20 minutes
Cooking time: 30 minutes

2 tbsp olive oil

500 g/1 lb 2 oz lean lamb fillet, thinly sliced

2 onions, sliced

2 garlic cloves, chopped

1 cinnamon stick

1 tsp ground ginger

1 tsp paprika

½ tsp chilli powder

600 ml/1 pint hot chicken stock

3 carrots, thinly sliced

2 turnips, halved and sliced

400 g/14 oz canned chopped tomatoes

25 g/1 oz raisins

425 g/15 oz canned chickpeas, drained and rinsed

3 courgettes, sliced

125 g/4½ oz fresh dates, halved and stoned or 125 g/4½ oz ready-to-eat dried apricots

salt

300 g/10½ oz couscous

600 ml/1 pint boiling water

1 Heat the oil in a frying pan and fry the lamb briskly for 3 minutes until browned. Remove the meat from the pan with a slotted spoon or fish slice and reserve.

2 Add the onions to the frying pan and cook, stirring, until softened. Add the garlic and spices and cook for 1 minute.

3 Add the stock, carrots, turnips, tomatoes, raisins, chickpeas and lamb. Cover, bring to the boil and simmer for 12 minutes.

4 Add the courgettes and dates and season to taste with salt. Cover again and cook for 8 minutes.

5 Meanwhile, place the couscous in a bowl with 1 teaspoon of salt and pour over the boiling water. Leave to soak for 5 minutes, then fluff with a fork.

6 To serve, pile the couscous onto a warmed serving platter and make a hollow in the centre. Place the meat and vegetables in the hollow and pour over some of the sauce. Serve the rest of the sauce separately, in a jug.

COOK'S TIP

Although chopping canned whole tomatoes may seem sensible as it is more economical, this will affect the final result. Whole tomatoes are always more watery, while chopped canned tomatoes have a more concentrated flavour.

main courses

Jambalaya

Inspired by another international favourite, paella, jambalaya is a speciality of New Orleans and its name is thought to come from the Spanish word for ham, jamón. There are also as many different versions of this Cajun dish, such as this one with chicken, as there are of its Spanish forebears.

SERVES 4

Preparation time: 20 minutes
Cooking time: 1–1¼ hours
Standing time: 10 minutes

3 tbsp vegetable oil

900 g/2 lb skinless, boneless
chicken thighs

1 onion, finely chopped

2 red or green peppers,
deseeded and finely chopped

2 garlic cloves, very finely
chopped

300 g/10½ oz long-grain rice

2 tbsp tomato purée

1 tsp dried thyme

1 tsp dried oregano

¼ tsp dried red chilli flakes

225 g/8 oz chorizo sausage,
cut into chunks

3 plum tomatoes, roughly
chopped

600 ml/1 pint hot chicken stock

3 spring onions, green part
included, finely chopped

salt and pepper

1 Heat the oil in a flameproof casserole over a medium–high heat. Cook the chicken in batches until lightly browned, stirring frequently. Remove with a slotted spoon and transfer to a plate.

2 Reduce the heat to medium. Add the onion and peppers and cook for 5 minutes, or until softened. Add the garlic and cook for 1 minute. Add the rice and cook for 5 minutes, stirring constantly.

3 Add the tomato purée, thyme, oregano, chilli flakes, chorizo and tomatoes. Season to taste with salt and pepper. Cook for 2–3 minutes.

4 Return the chicken and any juices to the casserole. Stir in the hot stock. Bring to the boil, then cover tightly and simmer over a low heat for 20–25 minutes, or until the rice is tender.

5 Remove from the heat. Sprinkle with the spring onions. Cover and leave to stand for 10 minutes before serving.

COOK'S TIP
Chorizo is a fairly spicy sausage that originated in Spain. Although all are made from pork and flavoured – as well as coloured – with paprika, there are many different varieties, some of which are quite mild and others of which are hot. You cannot tell them apart by their appearance. There are two types – ready-to-eat chorizo, which needs no further cooking, and cooking chorizo, which does. Either can be used in this recipe.

"Maybe Cajun cooking was the last great food secret to be revealed but it sure was worth waiting for." *Tim, Worcester*

main courses

Thai red curry

Thailand's vibrant cuisine, especially its aromatic and often quite hot curries, has certainly found its way into British hearts. Apart from the flavour, the difference between red and green curry pastes is that the former is made with red chillies and turmeric and the latter with green chillies and lime.

SERVES 4

Preparation time: 30 minutes
Cooking time: 40 minutes

6 garlic cloves, chopped

2 fresh red chillies, chopped

2 tbsp chopped fresh
  lemon grass

I tsp finely grated lime rind

I tbsp chopped fresh
  kaffir lime leaves

I tbsp Thai red curry paste

I tbsp coriander seeds,
  toasted and crushed

I tbsp chilli oil

4 skinless, boneless chicken
  breasts, sliced

300 ml/10 fl oz coconut milk

300 ml/10 fl oz chicken stock

I tbsp soy sauce

55 g/2 oz shelled unsalted
  peanuts, toasted and ground

3 spring onions, diagonally sliced

I red pepper, deseeded and sliced

3 Thai aubergines, sliced

2 tbsp chopped fresh Thai basil
  or fresh coriander

chopped fresh coriander,
  to garnish

freshly cooked jasmine rice,
  to serve

COOK'S TIP
Ready-made Thai curry pastes are of generally good quality, but it is also easy to make your own. Place 6 deseeded red chillies, I chopped garlic clove, 2 finely chopped shallots, I chopped lemon grass stalk, 4 black peppercorns, 2 coriander roots, I lime leaf, ½ tsp ground turmeric, ½ tsp coriander seeds, ½ tsp cumin seeds, ½ tsp shrimp paste, ½ tsp salt and a small pinch of ground cinnamon in a mortar. Grind with a pestle until smooth and combined. Gradually work in I tbsp groundnut oil. Spoon into a clean, screw-top jar and store in the refrigerator.

1 Place the garlic, chillies, lemon grass, lime rind, lime leaves, curry paste and coriander seeds in a food processor and process until the mixture is smooth.

2 Heat the oil in a preheated wok or large frying pan over a high heat, add the chicken and garlic mixture and stir-fry for 5 minutes. Add the coconut milk, stock and soy sauce and bring to the boil. Reduce the heat and cook, stirring, for a further 3 minutes. Stir in the ground peanuts and simmer for 20 minutes.

3 Add the spring onions, pepper and aubergines and simmer, stirring occasionally, for a further 10 minutes. Remove from the heat and stir in the basil and garnish with coriander. Serve immediately with freshly cooked jasmine rice.

main courses

Pad thai

This is Thailand's answer to chow mein, but, although they are both a combination of stir-fried noodles, vegetables and meat or prawns, the results are astonishingly different. The signature ingredients, lime juice, fish sauce and chilli, provide the uniquely delicious flavours.

SERVES 4

Preparation time: 20 minutes
Soaking time: 20 minutes
Cooking time: 15 minutes

225 g/8 oz rice noodles

90 g/3¼ oz peanuts, roughly
  chopped

2 tbsp lime juice

1 tbsp caster sugar

6 tbsp Thai fish sauce

1 tsp hot chilli sauce, to taste

250 g/9 oz firm tofu (drained
  weight), cubed

vegetable oil, for deep-frying

3 tbsp peanut oil

1 garlic clove, crushed

1 onion, finely sliced

1 red pepper, deseeded and
  thinly sliced

250 g/9 oz skinless, boneless
  chicken breast, cut into
  thin strips

85 g/3 oz beansprouts

125 g/4½ oz mangetout

175 g/6 oz cooked peeled
  prawns, cut in half lengthways

3 eggs, beaten

TO GARNISH

1 lemon, cut into wedges

4 spring onions, finely chopped

2 tbsp chopped peanuts

1 tbsp chopped fresh basil

1 Soak the noodles in a bowl of warm water for about 20 minutes, or until soft. Drain thoroughly in a colander and reserve. Mix the peanuts, lime juice, sugar, fish sauce and hot chilli sauce together in a small bowl and reserve.

2 Rinse the tofu in cold water, place between layers of kitchen paper and pat dry. Heat the oil for deep-frying in a large frying pan or wok. Deep-fry the tofu over a medium heat for 2 minutes until light brown and crisp. Remove from the heat, lift the tofu out with a slotted spoon and leave to drain on kitchen paper.

3 Heat another large frying pan or preheated wok and add the peanut oil, garlic, onion, red pepper and chicken strips. Cook for 2–3 minutes. Stir in the beansprouts and mangetout and cook for 1 minute. Then add the prawns, noodles, eggs and tofu and stir-fry for 4–5 minutes. Finally, add the peanut and lime juice mixture and cook for 3–4 minutes. Transfer to warmed dishes, garnish with the lemon, spring onions, peanuts and basil and serve.

COOK'S TIP

Made from rice flour and water, rice noodles may be bought dried or fresh. Dried noodles keep well in an airtight container. Fresh noodles should be used within 1 day of purchase. Usually sold in bundles, they are available in a range of widths from very thin vermicelli to flat ribbons.

"It's a cheeky dessert for me – I would steal ten minutes to myself just to indulge and savour every spoonful, and not share it!" *Sharon, Coatbridge*

desserts

Banoffee pie

Boston is not just the 'home of the bean and the cod' but also of this spectacularly rich pie. Its name indicates a melding of banana and toffee, so hardly surprisingly it is only for the really sweet-toothed — of which there seem to have been many among the voters.

SERVES 4

Preparation time: 20 minutes
Cooking time: 2¼ hours
Cooling time: 1–1½ hours

2 x 400 ml/14 fl oz cans
   sweetened condensed milk
6 tbsp butter, melted, plus
   extra for greasing
150 g/5½ oz digestive biscuits,
   crushed into crumbs
50 g/1¾ oz almonds, toasted
   and ground
50 g/1¾ oz hazelnuts, toasted
   and ground
4 ripe bananas
1 tbsp lemon juice
1 tsp vanilla essence
75 g/2¾ oz chocolate, grated
450 ml/16 fl oz thick double
   cream, whipped

1 Place the cans of condensed milk in a large saucepan and cover them with water. Bring to the boil, then reduce the heat and simmer for 2 hours. Ensure the water is topped up regularly to keep the cans covered. Carefully lift out the hot cans and leave to cool.

2 Preheat the oven to 180°C/350°F/Gas Mark 4. Grease a 23-cm/9-inch loose-bottomed flan tin with butter. Place the remaining butter in a bowl and add the biscuits and nuts. Mix together well, then press the mixture evenly into the base and sides of the tin. Bake for 10–12 minutes, remove from the oven and leave to cool.

3 Peel and slice the bananas and place them in a bowl. Sprinkle over the lemon juice and vanilla essence and mix gently. Spread the banana mixture over the biscuit crust in the tin, then open the cans of condensed milk and spoon the contents over the bananas. Sprinkle over 50 g/1¾ oz of the chocolate, then top with a thick layer of whipped cream. Scatter over the remaining chocolate, transfer to a plate and serve.

desserts

Fruit cheescake 2

There are dozens of different cheesecakes and pretty much all of them are irresistible, but this is one of the best and most popular combinations. The slight astringency of pineapple cuts through the richness of creamy filling to create a wonderfully refreshing end to a meal.

SERVES 4

Preparation time: 20 minutes
Chilling time: 4 hours

115 g/4 oz digestive biscuits, finely crushed
4 tbsp butter, melted, plus extra for greasing
100 g/3½ oz caster sugar
juice of 1 lemon
2 tbsp grated lemon rind
350 g/12 oz cream cheese
350 g/12 oz curd cheese
150 ml/5 fl oz double cream, whipped
400 g/14 oz canned pineapple slices, drained and halved
pinch of freshly grated nutmeg, to decorate (optional)

1 Place the crushed biscuits in a large bowl and mix in the melted butter. Grease a 20-cm/8-inch loose-bottomed cake tin with butter, then press the biscuit mixture evenly over the base.

2 Place the sugar in a separate bowl and stir in the lemon juice and the lemon rind. Add the cheeses and beat until thoroughly combined. Fold in the cream. Spread the cream mixture evenly over the biscuit layer. Cover with clingfilm and place in the refrigerator to chill for at least 4 hours.

3 Remove the cheesecake from the refrigerator, turn out onto a serving platter and spread the pineapple slices over the top. Sprinkle over a little grated nutmeg, if using. Serve immediately.

" Always was my fave dessert — and was often used as blackmail to make me eat my main course! "

Claire, Preston

"My wife's American and pecan pie is her answer when accusations fly about burgers and fries - and she's certainly won some hearts and minds." *Tom, Fulham*

desserts

Pecan pie

Dessert pies have a starring role in American cooking and this superb confection with its sweet, sticky nut and chocolate filling is an international success story. Go completely OTT and serve it with lashings of cream for a marvellously indulgent treat.

SERVES 4

Preparation time: 25 minutes
Chilling time: 45 minutes
Cooking time: 55–60 minutes
Cooling time: 15 minutes

PASTRY

125 g/4½ oz plain flour, plus
  extra for dusting
35 g/1¼ oz caster sugar
100 g/3½ oz unsalted butter,
  diced, plus extra for greasing
1 tbsp water

FILLING

125 ml/4 fl oz clear honey
50 g/1¾ oz butter
50 g/1¾ oz brown sugar
2 eggs, beaten
2 tsp almond extract
85 g/3 oz shelled pecan nuts,
  halved
85 g/3 oz plain dark chocolate,
  chopped

unsweetened cocoa powder,
  to decorate
single cream, to serve

1 To make the pastry, place the flour and sugar in a bowl and mix well. Rub in the butter, then stir in enough water to make a smooth dough. Form into a ball, wrap in foil and chill for 45 minutes.

2 Preheat the oven to 190°C/375°F/Gas Mark 5. Grease a 20-cm/8-inch loose-bottomed flan tin. Roll out the dough on a lightly floured work surface and use it to line the tin. Prick the base with a fork, line with greaseproof paper and fill with baking beans. Bake in the oven for 15 minutes.

3 Remove from the oven, then remove the paper and beans.

4 To make the filling, heat the honey, butter and brown sugar in a small saucepan over a low heat, stirring, until melted. Remove from the heat and leave to cool slightly, then beat in the eggs. Stir in the almond extract, nuts and chocolate. Pour the filling evenly into the pastry case, then bake in the oven for 40–45 minutes.

5 Remove from the oven and leave to cool for 15 minutes. Turn out onto a plate, dust with cocoa powder and serve with the cream.

COOK'S TIP

Pecan nuts are grown throughout the north-eastern United States, although this classic recipe comes from Mississippi. They are related to the hickory, but the kernel resembles the walnut in appearance and flavour. They have a very sweet flavour when fresh, but the dried nuts are less appealing.

desserts

Tarte citron

This classic French dessert looks so modest and unassuming that the unwary are completely unprepared for the magical contrast of textures and the explosion of flavour when they bite into it. Those in the know cast their enthusiastic votes for it.

SERVES 4

Preparation time: 25 minutes
Resting time: 30 minutes
Cooking time: 1 hour
Cooling time: 45 minutes

PASTRY

200 g/7 oz plain flour, plus extra for dusting

3 tbsp ground almonds

100 g/3½ oz butter, diced, plus extra for greasing

50 g/1¾ oz icing sugar, sifted

finely grated rind of 1 lemon

1 egg yolk, beaten

3 tbsp milk

FILLING

4 eggs

250 g/9 oz caster sugar

juice and finely grated rind of 2 lemons

150 ml/5 fl oz double cream

mascarpone or crème fraîche, to serve

1 To make the pastry, sift the flour into a bowl. Mix in the almonds, then rub in the butter. Mix in the icing sugar, lemon rind, egg yolk and milk. Knead briefly on a lightly floured work surface, then leave to rest for 30 minutes.

2 Preheat the oven to 180°C/350°F/Gas Mark 4. Grease a 23-cm/9-inch flan tin with butter. Roll out the pastry to a thickness of 5 mm/¼ inch and use to line the base and sides of the tin. Prick all over with a fork, line with greaseproof paper and fill with baking beans. Bake for 15 minutes. Remove from the oven. Reduce the oven temperature to 150°C/300°F/Gas Mark 2.

3 To make the filling, crack the eggs into a bowl. Whisk in the sugar, then the lemon juice and rind and cream. Spoon into the pastry case and bake for 45 minutes. Remove from the oven and leave to cool for 45 minutes. Serve the tart topped with mascarpone or crème fraîche.

COOK'S TIP

Pastry should always be allowed to rest for at least 30 minutes before it is rolled out. Roll it into a ball, wrap in clingfilm or foil and place in the refrigerator. It can be set aside to rest in any cold place, but extend the time to 1 hour. This helps it to develop its characteristic crisp texture during baking.

" We all got dazzled by French food and then disillusioned, so I really love it when people discover the casual understatement of this tart. "

Alison, Harrogate

Index